How to startup an Import/Export Business

1.0 The Import/Export Business

Import/export business is essentially buying a product in one country and selling it in another. This also applies to information and services. In other words, exports are products and services sold by individuals or nations while imports are products and services purchased. In United States alone, valued Products worth over a trillion dollars were exchanged last year and sales volumes are increasing every year. Now that we are in the information age with the Internet and World Wide Web services, I envisage a much more sales volume this year and in years to come. For this business, every buyer, manufacturer or Service Company in United States and the world, not already buying or selling overseas can be a potential client. Recent estimates indicate that there are nearly 40,000 non exporting American companies that could be exporting profitably to the rest of the world, and most of these are small businesses.

1.1 Trade

This means an exchange of Products and services for currency or Products and services offered by someone else. When this exchange takes place across national boundaries, it is called international trade.

1.2 Benefits

International trade is quite exciting and very rewarding. The thrill of completing your first transaction and the rewards or profit can be huge. There is a potential to make more commission on one good 'deal' than you would probably make in a month or a year throughout your career.

Apart from the income benefit, the possibility of trading with interesting and exotic countries, making contact with people from diversified background and nationalities, building your own international network and living a life that would be envied by many. If you have a taste for adventure then this is a great opportunity for you.

If you are not quite adventurous but want an admirable standard of living then this business is for you. It involves low risk and can be done without low capital requirement, you have little on-going costs except the cost of printed letter-headed paper, postage and phone cost, you do not need any stock to buy - you just arrange the deal and pick up your commission at the end of it. It is a form of business in which you can not only get staffed but also be successful if you are prepared to work at it.

You also do not have to be an expert or learn to speak foreign languages although that would probably help but you can succeed without all that. What you need is to have some basic knowledge, which you will find in this manual, a few initial contacts, and the determination to succeed - which is all up to you. A lot of people have done this over and over so you can be sure of success if you keep working at it the first two or people have done this over and over so you can be sure of success if you keep working at it the first two or three months, and if you are not earning a good income from commission within six months of starting, I will be very surprised.

1.3 Why People Export and Import Products or Services

1.3.1 Geographic Conditions

Some countries are geographically suited to the Production of certain Products, whereas others are not. For example, the United States cannot on a commercial basis produce cocoa owing to the absence of the required climatic conditions and yet we need large supplies of cocoa for chocolates, desserts and other kind of foods. Similarly, Japan has almost no natural reserves of oil and therefore has to import all of its requirements. This imbalance of the gifts of nature creates the need for an exchange of essential raw materials and Products created from those raw materials.

1.3.2 Costs of Production

If the cost of production per unit of product is cheaper in one country than in another (for example, because of lower labor costs) it will probably be more cost-effective for the second country to import that commodity (or item) than to produce it itself That is why some consumer products today are produced in Asia where labor costs are substantially lower than those in America.

1.3.3 Technology

In many countries there is a shortage of the essential resources necessary for the Production of high technology products. This may be raw materials, skilled labor or the specialized tools necessary for Production. These countries are therefore dependent upon supplies from those countries that can produce such Products or services (usually those with highly developed economies).

1.3.4 Economy of Scale

Another reason for trade between countries is the 'economy of scale'. This rule states that the cost of Production per unit decreases as the number of units produced increases until the most efficient level is achieved (the optimum point). Production can be increased in a number of ways: by the use of additional labor or raw materials or by finding more efficient methods of Production. It is therefore an advantage for a country to specialize in the Production of a certain commodity and then toad as supplier of that commodity to the rest of the world. For example, Australia specializes in the Production of wool and mutton; Japan specializes in the Production of electrical products such as televisions and computers. No country enjoys a monopoly of any of these items, each country's economy is a mixture of many Products and services, but most countries have at least one Product or service in which they specialize.

1.3.5 No Alternative

Some products or services have no domestic equivalent and hence all the demand for that commodity must be satisfied by importing from other countries. This applies especially to basic commodities and some high technology products. Many developing countries lack the skilled engineering labor with which to produce high-technology manufactured or consumer products for example machine tools and computers.

1.4 Similarities between International and Domestic Trade

Although much is made in the press and textbooks of the difference between overseas and domestic trade, little is ever said about the similarities. So let's have a quick look at these similarities:

1. By and large, the same Product is being sold with perhaps some local differences such as power supply.
2. The buyer abroad is going to use the Product for the same purposes as the domestic buyer, so they are not that different.
3. The supplier is usually going to be paid in his currency for an overseas order. The payment terms will probably be thirty days after date of invoice, the same as for

domestic trade. In fact he may receive payment much quicker through a letter of credit or bank draft.

The differences that exist are not an obstacle to overseas trade; they just require a little more care and attention to detail

1.5 Why Companies Enter International Trade

(a) To expand the business

Probably the most important reason for entering new markets overseas is to increase the business activity. For most companies there comes a time when the domestic market becomes saturation there is no more room left for market expansion, however most companies don't export because

- The company has no understanding of export markets; or has insufficient skilled staff to enter the international market. (The agent can offer his services in this regard.)
- The company's Products are not suitable for export, for technical reasons.
- The company is stagnating, needing a new driving force and ideas. (The agent can try to supply some of these ideas.)
- The company has insufficient capacity for export Production.

(The agent must try to encourage the company to invest in its future and its growth into the global market.)

Tens of thousands of small to medium size companies do not have such a formalized organization for handling exports and imports. They will tend to rely heavily upon the expertise of commission agents as they do not have their own expertise in-house. This is where you should seek new avenues of business for your agency.

1.6 Definition of an Agent

(a) Simply stated, an agent is a person or company who carries out work on behalf of another (the Client) and introduces a third party to the Client to create a contract on behalf of the Client. The authorities of the agent maybe detailed in an agency agreement between Client and agent or merely exist by implication and custom.

(b) The agent is not actually a party to the sales contract between the supplier and buyer unless he or she purposely involves himself or herself in that contract. His/her liability (legal obligation) under the contract is therefore strictly limited.

(c) The agent is a point of contact between the buyer and seller (importer and exporter), and represents the interests of one party (the Client) to the other. He or she is, therefore, an essential part of the contract.

You, as agent, save the buyer or supplier the considerable expense and complexity of setting up their own organization in the territory you cover.

1.7 The Commission Agent

The features of this type of agent are:

*You act on behalf of the Client and safeguard his interests. In return for this you will receive an agreed percentage of commission from the Client for all business you obtain on his behalf In addition, you may be granted a sole agency, for instance you have exclusive rights of sale in that territory, or that market for a particular Product. This means that you will gain commission on all sales for that Product even if they are placed direct with the Client.

* The Client is the person or company who you represent and on behalf of whom you act. He is usually the supplier of the Products you are selling. Sometimes, however, your Client can be the buyer. In this case you are finding Products on behalf of the buying party and you receive a commission from the buyer for performing this task. This situation is much less common than the more traditional supplier-agent relationship. Agents who find specific supplies for buyers are termed 'buying agents'

* The agent does not usually buy or sell the Products on his own behalf therefore he has no financial commitment to the sales contract, other than the value of his commission. The buyer pays the supplier directly by means of the agreed payment terms for the contract. This is why the agent does not need large capital resources to engage in this business.

* Your commission is paid by the Client, usually expressed as a percentage of the invoice value of the Products or services supplied under the contract. As soon as the contract is successfully completed and the supplier (your Client) receives his payment for the Products (or if you are acting as a 'buying agent', when the buyer receives the Products) you will be paid your agreed commission.

The commission agent has been part of international trade almost as long as there has been trade between nations without agents in world trade it is certain that the levels of trade would be significantly reduced as many suppliers and buyers would be unwilling to enter international trade without the assistance of an agent.

1.7.1 Functions of Commission Agent
You, as agent, fulfill a number of important functions:

(a) Your primary purpose is to obtain orders for the Products or services of your Client. In this regard you are usually appointed to cover a specific range of Products, in a specific geographical area. For example, porcelain Products from Taiwan into the US, or pharmaceutical Products from France to Brazil.

(b) You may be asked to carry out promotion for your Clients Products within the specified territory and market. This will involve the use of the supplier's promotional literature as well as any material produced by you. Often the Client will make full contribution to the cost of such material. You should follow up any leads that are generated by this activity.

(c) If the customer agrees to purchase Products then you will pass this order back to your Client for action. Usually you will check the order to ensure it is correct before forwarding it to the Client. Once the Client receives this order all further activity on the contract will be conducted directly between him and the buyer with you taking an advisory role while being kept informed of progress on the transaction. It is the responsibility of the Client to keep you informed, although often you will receive information from the buyer as well.

However, m some cases you may take more than just an advisory role in the fulfillment of the contract. You may handle any further correspondence with the third party (for instance the buyer),

- Co-ordinate the shipping arrangements (usually through a shipping agent) on behalf of the Client (for instance the supplier),
- Ensure that the shipping documents are correct.

If you are to fulfill these additional activities then you will normally receive a higher rate of commission. The commission agent does not usually get involved in the physical handling of the Products. However, you may assist with the shipping arrangements as stated above,

Some agents are authorized to perform after-sales service for the customers, especially if the Product is of a technical nature and customer support is an important issue. This may involve installation of the equipment, servicing or maintenance. You should only enter into agreements to carry out this sort of service if you are qualified so to do, or if you can find an associate company/contractor who can act on your behalf

1.8 Export Agents

The export commission agent acts on behalf of a supplier, the Client. The supplier may reside in the country of the agent, for example a US export agent may sell Products supplied by a United states manufacturer into a specific market, for example Britain. Or the supplier may reside m an overseas country, for example a United states export agent may sell Products supplied by an Indian manufacturer into a specific market, for instance Canada. In both of these cases the agent is acting as an export agent that means he is involved in the outward movement of Products from a supplier.

1.9 Import Agents

Import agents have the same relationship with their Client as do export agents but differ in that they are involved in the inward movement of Products from a supplier. In this case the example as above could be a commission agent in United States (or in Germany, or in Italy and soon) selling Products supplied by a Japanese manufacturer into the Canadian market (or the German or the Italian market respectively).

1.10 Buying Agents

The buying commission agent is less common than the selling commission agent. The responsibility of a buying agent is to find sources of supply for his Client. The Client in this case is the buyer. The agent will represent the buyer and will seek the required Products at the most competitive price. He may represent a particular territory, for instance Singapore, or South America, or group of Products, for instance cane furniture, or motorcycle parts, or he may be free to seek supplies anywhere. He receives a commission from the Client in the same way as a selling commission agent.

1.11 Creating International Trade Opportunities

As well as taking advantage of existing areas of international trade, for those companies that are already exporting or importing, the agent can also create new markets, Many companies never even think of entering international trade, instead concentrating all their efforts on their domestic trade as mentioned above, This is a good opportunity for the resourceful agent.

If you are offering to sell the Products of a supplier then he has nothing to lose by entrusting you with the sale if he currently does not achieve sales in that market. By concentrating all your energies on the sale of his Products you are going to prove successful for him and the relationship will grow from there.

Initially you need to find companies that are not currently exporting. How do you go about this?

* Look through your phone book and list any local companies that manufacture Products, for example a local chinaware manufacturer. Phone, or write, explaining that you are an export-import agent and that you are keen to find new Products for export markets. If they are already exporting then you may receive a negative answer. However, if they are not currently exporting it is quite likely that they will be interested in talking to you. This will hopefully lead to a meeting where you can find out about the Products they manufacture as well as the company itself This manual will enable you to handle this meeting with confidence.

* Alternatively, if you already know of companies or individuals who may be interested in exporting then contact them first - it's always easier to contact someone you know. When you have obtained this information you can research likely markets for the Product and start promotional activity faster.

When you communicate with these companies you will need to stress the benefits of overseas trade and offer your services in finding new international outlets for their Products. Most people are receptive to ideas that will benefit their business through selling their Product or service so your task will not prove that difficult.

Remember also that you can promote trade between other countries outside of your country; it isn't just trade between your country and another country that you need to consider. You need to continually research all the available outlets for information to see what buyers and suppliers are looking for so that any opportunities to put the two together are spotted and taken advantage of

Although above we are referring to manufacturers this is not the sole source of imported or exported products. You can act as agent for wholesalers, or even retailers.

2.1 Starting your Business

You can act as an import or export agent quite successfully as an individual, and there are advantages to this as outlined in the sole proprietorship section below. You certainly do not need to spend large sums of money when you start up, $300 would be useful but you might even manage with less, The essential things you will need to start up are:

(a) Letter-headed paper and matching envelopes. This is necessary for writing letters to prospective suppliers and buyers. It certainly looks better if you have a proper printed letter-head rather than plain paper. We cover this subject in detail later in this chapter.

(b) A computer with modem, Internet access, printer, word processing and fax software. Alternatively a portable, manual typewriter is also quite adequate to start with.

(c) Access to a phone so that you can make and take calls from prospective buyers and suppliers if required. International calls are expensive and should be avoided if possible –use e-mail, letter or fax instead,

You can manage this business from home using the Kitchen table as your desk so there is no reason why with the help of this manual you cannot start work today. This manual will give you all the information that you will need to start up your agency.

2.1 Choosing a Business Name

It is useful to add some form of description after your name to give an indication of the nature of your business, for instance Larry and sons International Sales Agent (or export-import Agent or international Trading specialist) or the name can be made up. It is usual to use last name in partnership trading names. the name of the owner and his business address must appear on any business stationery, letters and invoices.

2.2 What Form of Business?

You must now make a decision as to the precise nature of the business you will operate. The forms of business ventures that can be used are:

A. Sole Proprietorship

In a sole proprietorship, the business is owned and controlled by individual. This person alone receives the profits and takes the losses from the business; this person alone is responsible for the debts and obligations of the business. Income expenses of the business are reported on the proprietor's individual income tax return, profits are taxed at the proprietor's individual income tax rate. It is the simplest form of business structure you do need to register the name if it's different from your real name. I would recommend giving a potential client some idea of what it is that you do from the moment he picks up your business card. You also will need an account book to record transactions.

The account book is also useful when you come to complete your tax return. These can be purchased from any stationery shop for a relatively small sum. You don't need to understand accountancy to fill in one of these books. All you need to do is list all your revenue on one side of the book, for instance everything you earn. On the other side you list all your expenditure, for instance everything you have to pay out in the business. Keep all documents relating to these transactions, for instance invoices, receipts, check stubs and bank account statements, as these may be needed when you do your tax return?

You will also need a bank account in the name of your business. The bank account will be useful for paying expenses of the business by check and for depositing the commissions that you earn. However, the bank may charge for transactions on this type of account, so check first. A brief phone call to your local bank will give you the necessary information, it is important to understand that a sole trader has full responsibility for both the running of and the debts of the business.

B. Partnership

A general partnership is a business owned by two or more persons who associate to carry on the business as a partnership. Partnerships have specific attributes, which are defined by statute. All partners share equally in the right, and responsibility, to manage the business, and each partner is responsible for all the debts and obligations of the business. Distribution of profits and losses, allocation of management responsibilities, and other issues affecting the partnership usually are defined in a written partnership agreement. The partnership itself is not a taxable entity, but income and expenses of the partnership are reported on federal and state information" tax returns, which are filed by the partnership. The partners are taxed on their respective share of the partnerships profits at their individual income tax rates. An entity may be considered a partnership for tax purposes but not for other purposes.

A general partnership may convert to a limited liability partnership by filing a limited liability partnership registration. In limited liability partnerships, the personal assets of the partners are shielded against responsibility for some of the partnerships debts and obligations. It should be noted that limited liability partnerships are a new type of entity and all aspects, such as tax aspects, of such entities are not fully understood.

A limited partnership is a type of partnership in which the limited partners share in the partnership's liability only up to the amount of their investment in the limited partnership. By statute, the limited partnership must have at least one general partner and one limited partner. The general partner has the right and responsibility to control the limited partnership, and is responsible for the debts and obligations of the limited partnership. The limited partner, in exchange for limited liability, gives up the right to participate in the day-to-day management and control of the business. Limited partnerships must be established in compliance with statutory requirements, including requirements of tax and securities laws. Because of their complex nature, limited partnerships should not be undertaken without competent professional advice.

There are a number of advantages to this type of business structure:

- It is often more enjoyable working in partnership with someone else, especially if that person's skills complement your own, for example you have the ideas', but your partner is good at administering those ideas and bringing them to fruition.
- Any costs can be shared when you start up the business.
- You have someone to cover for you when you are on vacation or sick.
- You can share the workload.

You need to ensure that you have a sound agreement in writing with your partners. Such an agreement can be put together for you by an Attorney or, if it is straight forward, can also be worked out with your partner and then reviewed by an Attorney without very much cost.

In any partnership it is important that the partners have confidence in each other and contribute equally to the business.

C. Limited Liability Company

A business also may organize as a limited liability company. A limited liability company is a type of business organization that is designed to combine the tax treatment of a partnership with the limited liability characteristics of a corporation.

A corporation is a separate legal entity. It is owned by one or more shareholders. The corporation must be established in compliance with the statutory requirements of the state of incorporation. The shareholders elect a board of directors which has responsibility for management and control of the corporation. Because the corporation is a separate legal entity, the corporation and not its shareholders generally are responsible for the debts and obligations of the business. In most cases, shareholders are insulated from claims against the corporation.

This is Us !!

The corporation, as a separate legal entity, is also a separate taxable entity. The corporation may be taxed under Subchapter C of the Internal Revenue Code (a "C corporation") or Subchapter S of the Code (an "S corporation"). A C corporation reports its income and expenses on a corporation income tax return and is taxed on its profits at corporation income tax rates. The corporation income tax is also called a corporate franchise tax. Profits are taxed before dividends are paid. Dividends are taxed to shareholders, who report that as income, resulting in "double taxation' of profits which are paid as dividends. If the corporation meets the statutory requirements for S corporation status, the shareholders may elect to be taxed as an S corporation. Under the Internal Revenue Code, an S corporation may have only one class of stock, no more than 35 shareholders, and no shareholders that are nonresident aliens or non-individuals (for instance, corporations, partnerships, limited liability companies) except for certain estates and trusts. The S corporation is taxed in much the same manner as a partnership, for instance, the S corporation files an information return to report its income and expenses, but it generally is not separately taxed. Income and expenses of the S corporation "flow through' to the shareholders in proportion to their shareholdings, and profits are taxed to the shareholders at their individual tax rate.

It will take weeks to set up such a company or corporation (unless it is already made) but you are better protected in the long run. I've found that operating under a sole proprietorship or operating as a partnership makes more sense than incorporating an agency business. Why? Because the primary motive behind forming a corporation - which is a kind of artificial person from a legal standpoint - is to construct an entity that absorbs liability in the event of a lawsuit You don't make anything, you offer a service, the risks traditionally associated with Agency businesses are minimal Many agencies operate as sole proprietors or partnerships rather than corporations, especially if you intend importing or exporting products on your own account. However, a commission agency is not a high-risk business and this is not therefore such an important issue to consider initially.

2.3 Location

Regardless of the form of business adopted you can still run it from home. Every limited company must by law have a registered office and this can be your home address. However, if you don't want to use your home address, firms that offer company-formation facilities will provide such a service, but they will charge you a fee for this.

As your agency grows, you may well decide to obtain your own business location. You do not need any special type of office for a commission agency, providing it has a desk, a computer and a phone. You do not need any special location as most of your work will be done by correspondence and thus location is not of great importance. Contact your local estate agent for further details of what is available locally and what you will have to pay for it. Alternatively, watch the small ads in your local newspapers.

2.4 Business Address

Sometimes instead of using your own address on letterheads and for replies to correspondence you may prefer to use a mailbox address. This service is offered by companies and individuals. In principle it works as follows. You use the mailbox address on your correspondence instead of your own, the correspondence received at this address is forwarded to you and a fee is charged for the use of this service. The advantage of this system is that your own address, especially if it is your private residence, is not known to the people with whom you are dealing and hence you will not get callers coming to your home. You will find these types of services listed in your local business phone book, under private mailboxes heading.

If you do decide to physically handle your Client's Products, either as an
On consignment agent or to resell at a profit, then you may also need storage Facilities. These can be rented or leased in the same way as an office; alternatively, you could pay a local storage company to keep the products

A note of caution, if you are living in rented accommodation you may need the landlord's permission before using the location for business purposes. Similarly, if you are living in owned accommodation you may need the local authority's permission

2.5 How to Communicate Internationally

(a) Written correspondence

Initially, all you will need are 500 letter-headed sheets of paper for writing letters to prospective suppliers and buyers. This represents an economic quantity. Use a good quality paper as this will improve the image of your business. Make sure that you choose envelopes that match the color and size of your letter-heads.

The letter-head should contain your name, and business name, your full address, your phone number and your fax number. You might also like to mention the nature of your business, for instance import-export Agent. Manufacturer's Agents. If you are a limited company then additional information may be required, such as the address of your registered office and your company registration number.

Business cards are useful if you are going to visit any of your Clients or buyers; you can then give them a card to keep for future reference.

These items can be printed at any printing shop in about a week, maybe less. The cost varies for 500 letter size letter-headed sheets. The more established printing companies are usually more expensive and take a little longer but the end Product is often of a better quality. You do not need any special design; your printer will assist you with advice on this.

You do not need to produce special invoice forms at this stage; you can easily use a letter-head with INVOICE printed or typed across the top if you do have to raise an invoice for your commission or any direct trading you maybe doing.

TIP If you have a good quality printer and a computer, you could buy any software that can effectively produce good quality letterheads and business cards. The Business card paper and letter size sheets can easily be purchased at any office supplies outlet. Remember that your stationery is an advertisement for your business - use it wisely.

(b) Phone

You may need a phone as your business grows. Initially you can make use of your existing home line to receive and make occasional calls. If you find that the number of calls you make and receive justifies it, and if your revenue allows it, it may be wise to rent a separate business line.

(c) Fax

The use of the fax as a means of business communication is growing at a rapid rate. A fax transmits a picture' of a document from you to the receiver through conventional phone lines. If you have fax software a scanner and a modem, you do not need to purchase a fax machine. Alternatively if you look in your local phone book you will find copy centers that provide a fax service to local businesses.

(d)   Telex

Access to a telex facility can prove an invaluable tool in international trade. A telex consists of a visual display unit with keyboard and printer that transmits written messages to other telex users throughout the world.

There are administrative services that offer telex facilities, and using such a service will prove cheaper, especially if you are an infrequent user. You simply state your message by phone and they send the telex for you. They will also take your incoming telexes for you.

(e)   e-mall

E-mail is a priceless instrument in international trade. It works on the same principle as letters except that you receive written messages. There are a number of other advantages in using the e-mail as a means of communication: It is cheaper than the phone word for word and you have a written record of what has been said

TIP: You should always state your Tax, phone and e-mail address on your business stationery.

Other Professional Services

Accountant

You do not need the services of an accountant to start up and run your agency business. However, you will need the services of an accountant when it comes to submitting your annual accounts to the tax authority this only applies if you are self-employed, or in partnership - limited companies have different considerations. Your annual accounts are the basis on profits you have made in your business.

Attorney

You can manage quite well without an Attorney, especially m the early stages. They really start to prove necessary when you are, for example, entering into a partnership agreement, or signing a lease for location. Having this type of written contract checked by an Attorney before signing gives greater peace of mind as they will spot any loopholes in the document. Attorney's fees, however, can be very expensive! Always ask the cost first before giving instructions to an Attorney.

Bank

You will need a bank account to operate your agency business and it is not a bad idea to build a good relationship with your bank manager as well. Go to see him and explain what you are intending to do with your business, he may be able to offer good advice as he is dealing with businesses every day. The right bank, and bank manager, can be invaluable to your business.

2.6 Organizing your Business

(a) Book keeping

You do not need to keep any complicated accounting books for your agency business. A simple account book such as you find at a local stationery office will be adequate. You do need to keep accurate and regular records for tax reasons. If you are a sole trader or partnership, then you will need to record the following in your account books:

- The amount of money, if any, that you put into the business.
- Any further money you spend on the business, such as stationery supplies. You must have receipts for these items. The first rule of having your own business is to get a receipt for everything you spend!
- Any loans taken out for the business.

- Any money you receive from commissions, when you received it and from where.
- A proportion of your expenditure on utility bills for example lighting, heating, mileage, phone calls and car expenses can be claimed as a business cost.

You will need to keep additional records for a limited company, such as records of director's meetings and a list of any shareholders in time business.

(b) Record-keeping

Apart from simple financial book-keeping it is also useful to keep a record of your sales that you achieve on your Client's behalf and the customers or buyers to whom you sell. Always keep your records up to date and in good order so that you can find things easily. A separate file for each of your Clients would be useful. All the correspondence that relates to that Client can be kept in date order in the file so that you have a complete history of his activity at your fingertips. This information can, of course, be kept on computer if you have access to one.

(c)　Skill

You can quite successfully run a small business single-handed with no requirement for staff. This is especially true of the agency business, as will be mentioned below. However, you may decide to recruit some form of assistant.

How do you go about this? First, try to get free help! Can your wife, son, daughter, brother or sister help you with your business either for free or for low cost? If not, you can use an administrative service center to help you? They will provide services on an 'as needed' basis at a rate of cost per hour, or per job. They offer services such as typing, mail boxes, addressing envelopes and sending faxes. You will find them listed in your local phone book.

If you decide to recruit staff because your level of work warrants it, the instance you cannot handle the workload single-handed any longer, then there are a number of ways to go about it:

(I) You can advertise directly in the classified 'recruitment' section in local newspapers. The cost is not that high depending upon the size and complexity of the advertisement. Replies can either be sent directly to your address or to the newspaper itself Suggested wording of the advert could be as follows:

PART-TIME ADMINISTRATIVE ASSISTANT required for export-import Agency. Candidates should be able to type, answer calls and carry out general office duties. Must be able to work on own initiative. Please call g88-8888 or Send your resumes to Harry and sons Agency (+address)

(2) You can recruit a 'temp (temporary member of staff) through an employment agency. There are usually several of these even in quite small towns. You tell them the type of person you are looking for and they will send along prospective recruits for you to interview. However, the cost of this service can be high because you don't just pay for their labor cost; you also pay the weekly agency fee on top of that, usually between 10 and 20 per cent of the employee's wages. The advantage of employing 'temps' is that you don't have to worry about things like employee taxes, health insurance and other issues..

TIP: We would recommend that you first run your business single-handed before starting to distribute your profits through pay packages.

3.0 Choosing a Product

Are you interested in the Product? If so, then that will probably help you to sell it. We all have interests or hobbies that we enjoy learning about and taking part in. If you can turn a hobby into a living then that will make your work both more enjoyable and more rewarding. If you are enthusiastic about, and believe in the Product then this will rub off on the prospective buyer. You need to be 'sold' on the Product if you are going to deal in it successfully.

3.1 Price

Nearly everything that you buy, or that can be bought, can be imported more cheaply from somewhere. Price has to be one of the most important factors influencing what you are going to sell. If you can undercut the price of existing Products on the market and yet provide a comparable quality of Product then you are bound to win over some buyers and achieve sales.

To establish how important this factor is you will need to find out two things:

1. The price that the item is currently selling for in the market
2. The price you can import the item for.

To establish this information you will need to do some research.

To discover the current selling price of the item may sound simple but nevertheless requires some thought. There is rarely just one price for an item; usually the Product will sell for different prices depending on a number of factors:

* Sales outlet. The nature of the sales outlet will have an effect upon the price. Products sell more cheaply in department stores than they do in small shops. Again, the Product may sell even more cheaply through mail order. You will need to check each type of outlet.

* Geography. Products may be more expensive in certain parts of the country. This could be because of additional transport costs or because of lower consumer demand in that area.

* Supply and demand Price tends to fluctuate in accordance with the laws of supply and demand. If the price is reduced then demand will tend to increase and vice versa.

Carefully check out these factors before establishing the lowest price for the Product, the average price for the Product and the highest price for the Product.

The second consideration is the price of the imported Product. To establish this you need the basic price of the item from the manufacturer plus the charges outlined below in the section entitled 'Importation'. Again the basic price will vary depending upon several factors:

* The supplier. Prices vary from one supplier to another depending upon their costs of manufacture and profit margins.

* The country of origin. Prices will also vary between different countries of origin. This needs to be checked so that you can establish the most competitive price.

* Quantity. Price will also vary with the quantity ordered. Generally speaking the more you order, the cheaper the unit price becomes.

Carefully research of these factors now will save you time and work later.

3.2 Competition

How strong are the competitors? Whatever Product you choose to sell, unless it is something absolutely new, there will be competition in the market place. However, there are a number of ways that you can set about to beat the competition.

1. Price

You find out what competitors are selling their Product for, as mentioned above, and undercut it. This, of course, is only valid if you can still cover your commission and enable the supplier to make a profit. Also it depends on the supplier (your Client) allowing you to reduce the price of his Product. Always seek his approval before changing the price.

2. Quality

If you can provide a higher quality Product, even at a slightly higher price, then you will gain buyers for the Product. Similarly, if your Product will do more, or last longer than competing Products, you will beat the competition. Customers are prepared to pay a premium for quality and service.

3. Added value

Value can be added to the Product. This can be done by better packaging, after-sales services or guarantees with each Product bought. Better packaging will make the Product more attractive, reduce the risk of damage and will act as an advertisement. After-sales services would include such items as installation of a piece of equipment, for instance a fridge/freezer or water filter; maintenance agreements for machinery; on-site training for the operators/users of the Product; technical hot-lines for customer inquiries and so on.

Guarantees covering the Product for a period of time promising to repair or replace the Product if it fails are a useful method of adding value.

4.   Increased promo/ion

You can put more effort into promoting your Product. The greater the amount of promotion, the greater the sales - this can be done by approaching a list of prospective buyers using effective advertising methods, such as direct mailing. It is generally true that your sales of the Product will be in direct proportion to the amount of effort you put into marketing the Product.

5. Selling methods

You can fly new ways of selling the Product. For example, through mail-order catalogues or by network marketing, methods that the competition may not have attempted. There are ways to fight the competition and win. Let us look at these alternatives in a little more detail:

* Mail-order catalogues

Home shopping has become a major method of Product distribution over the past 25 years. Most people have purchased a Product through a mail-order catalogue or in response to a newspaper/magazine advertisement. It is a very effective method of selling. It has the benefit of being convenient for the consumer It is also cost-effective for the supplier in that he does not require a retail location to attract his customers The costs of advertising are obviously higher, but even so it is a profitable method of retailing.

* Network marketing

This is a relatively new method of retailing. It has been used here for about thirty years on a wide range of consumer Products, and is a very successful method of retailing.

3.3 Market

The larger the market for a Product the easier it is to penetrate that market and take a small percentage of it. On the other hand, can you find a Product that will create its own market? In this age of high technology and mass Production there seems to be an endless supply of gadgets that nobody really needs but everybody buys! For example, did you know that there is a large international market in wooden, hand-painted ducks? Well, there is and it's very profitable. So when you are researching sources of supply look out for Products that aren't yet on sale in your country or the country you are selling to and see if you can develop a market People like novelty and innovative, new ideas.

3.4 Quality

Is the Product of a better quality, or of more advanced technology, than existing Products in the market? We have already touched on this issue of quality above. If you can market a Product which is stronger, faster, more attractive, quieter, smaller or whatever, than its main competitors then you will erode their market share and gain sales for yourself The consumer is always looking for an improved version of everything under the sun, even if the improvements seem quite trivial.

3.5 Technology

Do you understand the Product and its purpose? You are going to need at least a working knowledge of the Product and what it does if you are going to be able to talk to prospective buyers about it. This knowledge may well be provided by the supplier, either in the form of written material or by direct training.

Alternatively, get a book on the subject from your library and read up on it. It is important to gain this knowledge as it will assist you in conducting transactions and will also help your relationship with the supplier. Ins particularly important if you are going to be involved in providing any form of 'after-sales' service - for example, installation and maintenance of a piece of equipment. The general rule is the more knowledge the better - become an expert

3.6 Importation

Can the product be easily imported into the country of destination? There are a number of things to consider when importing Products from another country:

1. Freight cost

This, when added to the FOB (free on board the vessel or aircraft that carries the products) cost of the products can make the total price of the products unprofitable when compared with existing domestic Products. To keep freight costs under control remember the following guidelines:

Freight charges depend on volume as well as 'dead' weight, whichever is the greater. Always check both if you are responsible for the shipment or are calculating shipping costs for a customer. A shipping agent will be able to advise you in this regard, you will find them listed in the phone book.

Get competitive quotations from shipping agents. Rates may vary from agent to agent, often quite a lot. This occurs for a number of reasons: natural competition, or because one shipping agent maybe stronger in a particular region than another, or may offer a different route for the shipment.

Look at alternative methods of shipment.

    a) Is it cheaper to post it?

    b) Air freights it?

    c) Send it by road?

Usually a shipping agent will be able to calculate this for you and will give you the correct method of shipment for the consignment.

2. Import Duty and Taxes

These charges, if applicable, will be additional to the invoiced value of the products. These charges are imposed by Customs authority as a method of raising revenue for the government, and most countries have some similar form of taxation applying to imported products. It is also a way of protecting home-made products. The checks are usually payable at time of importation. These charges are the responsibility of the importer/buyer, not the agent. However, you need to be aware of them so that you can inform potential customers. You can obtain detailed information by:

1. Obtain a copy of Customs Tariff which contains details of every Product and its respective duty rate, if applicable. Your local Customs office will advise you on how to purchase a copy.

2. Calling the Customs office and ask them.. They are usually very helpful when you contact them. To be able to assist you they will need to know the following:

    (a)   The Product or industry in which you are interested.
    (b)   The country of export.
    (c)   The value or weight of products involved.

This will enable them to give you the specific duty rate for those particular products.

3. Import restrictions

Specific import licenses may be required for certain products for instance agricultural Products, foodstuffs or chemicals and so on. Some products may be completely banned.. Again, you can find out if this applies to the products from the customs office. It is particularly important that you check this out right at the start to avoid problems later.

4. Suitability

Is the Product suitable for the market? For example, some imported electrical appliances will not work here because of different voltages. Some toys do not conform to state regulations. You need to find out this information before importing the Product.

3.7 Exportation

If you are acting as an export agent you will need to clarification on certain issues before commencing your activity. You need to be sure that supplying this Product to the intended country of destination will be a worthwhile commercial proposition. What are the issues to be considered?

Cost

Simply stated, will the Product be price competitive in the intended market place? You can establish this by firstly finding out the price of the Product in the country abroad and then by establishing the price you will need to charge for your Product to cover the costs and make a profit. In most cases the manufacturer or supplier, your Client, will determine the selling price of The Product, but it is still useful for you to know how this is calculated.

To get the price, go to the reference section of the library m your area.. Look up the Product concerned in the classifications in international trade directories and this will give you the names and addresses of manufacturers and suppliers of the Product in the country you intend to export to. Write to these companies requesting price lists and brochures - this should give you all the information you will need

Secondly, you need to understand the way that the price of an exported Product is constructed. It is made up of a number of elements:

- Production costs - materials, labor, fuel and tools used to manufacture the Product.
- Profit - the percentage increase over Production costs that ensures a profit for the manufacturer.
- Insurance - the cost of insuring the Product while in transit.
- Freight - the cost of packing and shipping the Product.
- Import duty - the cost of any import duty levied by the country.
- Ancillary, for instance any other costs - for example delivery from the seaport or airport of arrival and storage.

The supplier can provide the first two items of information but he may require your assistance with establishing the other items. How can you do this? Again it is fairly simple. A shipping agent can provide all of the other items of information providing you can give him some basic information concerning the Product, such as size, weight, value and method of shipment required - all items that the supplier will be able to provide.

Once you have established these two prices - The cost of the domestic Product in the country of destination, and the cost of your Product when it arrives in the country of destination - you can judge whether your Product will be competitive.

2.   Import restrictions

Many other countries have similar restrictions. You can find out what these are by contacting the commercial section/office of the embassy or consulate of that country.

3.   Suitability

Is the Product suitable for the intended market? Does it comply with their safety and quality regulations? (Germany, for example, has quite strict regulations concerning safety and quality of Products.) If in doubt always check first by speaking to the commercial section of the embassy or consulate of the relevant country.

4.0 Product Research

4.1 Technical Specification

To promote a Product effectively you have to have some understanding of the nature of the Product and its uses. This knowledge does not have to be detailed but it does need to be adequate to answer the questions of prospective buyers. Most of this technical information will be provided by your client in the form of brochures, advertising literature and manuals.

However, it is useful to seek out as much information as you can on the Products you are going to promote. The more background knowledge you accumulate, the easier it will be to find buyers for the Product. How do you find this information? There are a number of ways:

(a)   Obtain a sample of the Product from your prospective supplier as soon as you possibly can, preferably before you sign the agency agreement (or agree to an agency by letter/fax) or take any orders from potential buyers. This is providing, of course, that it is not very expensive or an advanced technical or specialized Product. This will give you the chance to study the item, possibly even to use it, for this teaches you more than any amount of literature.

(b)   If the Product is of a technical or industrial nature then you may not be able to obtain a sample, but you can still watch a demonstration of the Product in use, or a video of it.

(c)   If neither of the above opportunities is available then at least study photographs, or the end Product of the piece of machinery, for example, in the case of a packaging machine, samples of the packaging that the machine produces. The prospective buyer is more likely to be interested in the results of the machine, for instance the packaging, than the detailed technical description of how it works.

(d)   Read the trade magazines for the industry concerned. These can be obtained through private subscription or occasionally free of charge if you are already involved in that particular industry. These magazines are not generally available from newsagents~ you receive them directly through the post when you subscribe. They usually contain reader-Inquiry cards for those seeking further information concerning the Products or companies advertised in the magazine.

4.2 Annual Sales of the Product

There are market research companies that track and publish this data on a regular basis bringing out monthly or quarterly reports; they can be found listed in the phone book. However the cost of using these companies can be quite high and we would not recommend this level of expenditure until your business is well established and can easily afford it. More specific information can be found in reference libraries. Be the first in the market - a very lucky position in which to find yourself.

4.3 Sales Channel

Another essential part of the picture is the channel (method) for selling used for the Product. At the sane time as you are researching the Product itself you need to find out the most effective method of marketing. You might ask yourself the following questions:

- Does it sell best through mail order catalogues?
- Malls and shopping centers?
- The conventional retail establishment seen in most towns and cities
- Through distributors?

The distributor effectively acts like a wholesaler, buying in quantity directly from the manufacturer and then on-selling at a profit to retailers

- Through dealers?

The dealer is in effect a retailer who will buy either directly from the manufacturer or through a distributor

- By direct promotion to industrial users?

This may be achieved by mail-shots or by the use of a direct sales force employed by the manufacturer.

- By network marketing?

   By using a large network of individuals each selling a small quantity of the
   Product directly to end-users

Understanding the sales channel will greatly assist you in achieving actual sales as you will approach the right people in the right way, rather than by trial and error.

The simplest way to find this out is to look at the home market first, that being the one that s most accessible to you.

4.4 Future Sales Trends

What does the future hold for the Product? By looking at the way past sales have moved you can judge the future trend as well. However, there are other considerations that may determine future sales of the Product. These might include

(a)   Improved Quality

If the quality of the Product is regularly improved then it is likely to influence future sales trends in a positive way.

(b)   Reduced prices

Similarly, reducing the selling price of the Product should have a positive influence on demand. Obviously the amount that the supplier can reduce the price is limited as he still has to cover all his costs, pay your commission and make a profit.

(c)   Technical advances

The rate of technological advance means that even quite ordinary Products are continually being improved, becoming easier to use, having added features and functionality. This may also have a positive influence on sales of the Product.

(d)   Competitive Products

The introduction of new competitive Products, or the improvement of existing competitors, may have an adverse effect upon the sales of your Product. In this case, in addition to improving quality the buyers could be offered some other form of incentive such as reduced prices or more Product for their money, or the Product could be 'positioned' in a different way so that It no longer appears to compete with the opposition. This can be done by taking, for example, a child's toy and calling it an 'educational aid' instead of a toy. This gives it an up-market and beneficial image, possibly pulling it ahead of the competition.

(e)   Better promotion

This is one of the most important factors in persuading a prospective buyer to purchase. If the promotion or advertising of your Product is good then your sales will reflect this. Good advertising not only pays for itself in increased sales, but contributes towards profit.

(/)   Better after-sales service

Offering the buyer a better deal on after-sales service, especially in the area of white goods (for instance microwaves, washing machines or ovens) and home appliances, will often steal the advantage over the competition.

(g)   Environmental aspects

Nowadays companies that manufacture Products that are better for the environment, or a have a 'greener' image, may have a sales advantage over their less 'environmentally friendly' competitors.

These factors show that future sales of your Product are determined by more than just historic patterns. You need to consider all of these factors when researching this area.

4.5 Details of Competitors

To find out about your competitors is not a difficult task. By competitors we mean those companies or individuals that are currently offering

Goods or services that compete with the Product you wish to promote. In that sense they are realty your supplier's competitors. Most of them will be advertising their Products openly if they want to achieve sales. To monitor your competitors you might do the following.

(a) Keep notes of this information when you see such advertising. The method of advertising may be newspapers, magazines, posters, radio, television or direct mail. Whichever method you come across make notes of the following points:

- Method of advertising
- Place of advertising
- Name and address of supplier
- Price of the Product
- Technical features, if any
- Benefits for the consumer
- Method of packaging

- Special offers, if any

(b) Send for their brochures and price list as these will teach you a great deal about both the Product and its market.

Other sources of such information are:

* Trade Directories

The trade directories available at public libraries will list most of the competitors, often giving fairly detailed information about them. The ones listing companies by industry grouping are particularly useful.

* Newspapers

These, apart from including advertisements for competing Products, also often include write-ups about companies. Further information is also given away when they advertise for staff in the recruitment sections.

4.6 Price of Competing Products

Once you have found the details of the competitors you can ask for their catalogues and price lists to compare with your own. This again is not a difficult task. Most companies' part with their price lists without a second thought - they are not particularly confidential.

The purpose of such comparison is to determine whether your Product is over-priced or wider-priced for the market. If your competitor has already announced his price then there is more room for movement with yours. One of the following options can be applied:

(a) Undercut the main competitor's price. This assumes that you have sufficient profit margin in the Product price to be able to do this.

(b)   Sell at a comparable price and compete on quality. This means that you highlight any differences or improvements in your Product compared to the competitors.

(c)   Sell at a higher price and thereby suggest (without actually saying whether or not it is) that your Product is of higher quality than the competitor's This can have its dangers, in that the customers may be very price sensitive and will immediately switch to the cheaper Product.

4.7 Product Promotion

You need to discover the most effective methods of promoting this Product so that any expenditure allocated to this area achieves the required results. At the end of the day you may need to experiment to find the most effective method. How do you do this?

*   Firstly, if you have already carried out the research mentioned above concerning how the competitors promote their Product, then you will have some of the answers. If the competition is successfully promoting the Product, for example electrical goods, by using distributors, then you would be wise to adopt a similar approach. There is no point in learning by trial and error if someone else has already had the lessons!

*   Secondly, ask the supplier how he promotes the Product in his own market. Generally speaking what is effective in one market will work in another. This is not always the case however.

*   Thirdly, look at similar Products and see how they are promoted.

Wherever possible get your client to find the cost of promotion either by providing the materials or by refunding any expenditure incurred by you. Most clients are helpful in this regard, although sometimes the supplier's advertising material is inadequate for the market concerned. This can be for a number of reasons, for example poor translation or inferior quality of printing. This necessitates the Production of your own material. What you need initially is some typed up, or possibly photocopied (good quality), price lists and photographs (in color where possible) of the Products, with a description of the Product underneath, including any necessary technical information. Later on you may want to produce your own leaflets. The cheapest way is to use a local printer, who will prepare the photographic work, design, artwork and printing for you.

4.8 Packaging and Presentation

You will need to research the various methods of packaging used for the Product.

* Do buyers expect to see it packed and presented for sale in a particular way? Presentation of the Product can have a major effect on sales. This is especially true of foodstuffs and consumer Products.

* Is the Product such that it must be specially packed to protect it or prevent it from leaking? Some Products, such as engineering equipment, may contain oil-based lubricants which act as irritants to the skin. Therefore precautions have to be taken to avoid spillage or leakage.

Visit existing outlets for the Product, if there are any, to establish what the industry standards are. If you are seeking to promote the Product overseas, then ask the embassy (commercial section) of the country concerned how the Product should be packed for sale in that country. This information will need to be relayed back to your client so that he can take the necessary action.

The choices of packaging are numerous: boxes, cartons, plastic, molded plastic, glass jars and bottles, paper bags and so on. The method of packing will depend upon the Product and the handlings it will receive between manufacture and purchase by the customer.

4.9 Quality Requirements

Another essential area of research is that of quality.

You need to check this on two fronts:

(a)   What is the standard quality of the Product on the market?

(b)   What is the quality of the Product you will be promoting?

In all probability there will be a number of Products on the market with varying degrees of quality. The quality of your Product will need to meet at least the minimum requirements of the market, for instance any requirement as to safety and standards compliance.

4.10 Safety Standards and Regulations

It is advisable to ensure that the Product is in every way, including the instructions for use, a suitable Product for The market concerned.

Basically there are two types of commission agent, those who are primarily involved in imported goods and those who are primarily involved in exported goods. It is worth noting that many agents act as both import and export agents and the two areas do not greatly differ.

If possible, you should look for opportunities in areas, importing and exporting, as this will maximize your agency potential. However, you may find you have a preference for one or the other, or you may end up doing one type of agency because that is the first business opportunity you find.

The import agent acts on behalf of an overseas supplier and will look after the interests of that supplier and will promote the sale of his goods in the home market,

5.0 Finding Suppliers

Obtaining an agency, even a sole agency, is not difficult. In fact, once your name becomes known you will get people contacting you offering agencies. No one is likely to object to you promoting their Products for them, or to paying you a commission for your service, unless they are already tied into a sole agency agreement with someone else. There is nothing to stop you contacting many different prospective suppliers covering many different Products.

5.0.1 Patents

This is occasionally a problem with some imported Products. There may be a registered patent on a Product already on sale in the market. If you are uncertain about a particular Product you can seek advice from the Patent Office before proceeding with the sale or promotion of the Product.

5.1 Embassies and Consulates

There is little difference between an embassy and a consulate and their function as far as commercial activity is concerned is identical. Every country has either an embassy or a consulate and you should contact whichever is available nearest to you.

You should write to these addressing your letter to the Commercial Section. A sample letter is drafted below for your assistance. Your letter should contain your full name and address. You should state clearly the nature of your business and in which Products you are interested. Alternatively, if your Inquiry is a of a general nature then state that you require basic information about the Products. For export goods it is best to contact the commercial section of the embassy concerned regarding the quality standards of the relevant country.

Sample contact letter to an embassy or consulate

MAXWELL IMPORT & EXPORT AGENCY

8992 West 89'" Street

Suite 001

Chicago IL 60S43

Phone (312) 567-8421

Fax (312) 568-8421

10 October, 2002

The Embassy of Belgium,

Commercial Section,

3330, Garfield Street NW,

Washington DC 20008

Dear Sirs,

Subject: Computer Components.

I am an import agent specializing in high-tech consumer products.

I would very much appreciate your assistance in finding Belgium

Suppliers of computer components for importation into Argentina. Would you please be kind

enough to send me the following information?

(a)   Details of available trade contacts I export offices

(b)   Suppliers names and details that you have on file

(c)   Product brochures that you have on file

(d)   Relevant trade associations that I may contact.

Could you also please add my name to your mailing list for this category of goods, and pass

my details back to the relevant trade body in Argentina.

I look forward to receiving the requested information and thank you for your assistance,

Yours faithfully,

(Signed)

Tom Maxwell

Maxwell import/Export Agency

* By adding your name to the mailing list of the embassy your details will be circulated to

many suppliers in the country concerned

Ask for trade directories, lists of manufacturers or exporters of the Product concerned, details of trade associations, trade magazines, and brochures and so on. Ask also to be added to their regular mailing list.

It may take a week or two before you receive a reply as the commercial staff of these embassies are often under considerable pressure from their substantial workload. It varies from embassy to embassy but don't be discouraged if you haven't received a reply after a couple of weeks, Nine times out often you will get a reply in the end. They will normally send all the material they have available that is relevant to your Inquiry. They will also often pass your name and details back to their own country for the reference of their manufacturers and suppliers. This often leads to letters directly from these manufacturers and suppliers a few weeks after your initial Inquiry to the embassy. You can also call them on phone or fax the letter if you can. If you have access to the internet, you can visit the embassy's home page and then sent the letter to the E-mail address. A combination of all these would produce results much faster

The trade magazines and other information received back from the commercial sections of embassies may list hundreds, or even thousands, of Products and their respective suppliers. The information is also usually provided free of charge.

5.2 Trade Associations
Trade associations will often be able to provide details of both corresponding associations overseas and also of overseas suppliers of The Product concerned. You can find the

names, addresses and phone numbers of trade associations in your local phone book or in the reference section of libraries, a phone call or a brief letter to the relevant body will often be enough to obtain the required information. A sample letter is given below.

Sample contact letter to a trade association

MAXWELL IMPORT & EXPORT AGENCY

8992 West 89th Street

Suite 001

Chicago IL 60643 U.S.A.

Phone (312) 568-8421

Fax (312) 568-8421

10 October 2002

Plastic Manufacturers Association,

Union Building,

Belgium

Dear Sirs,

Would you please provide ire with any details you may have on file regarding suppliers of Plastic recycled materials. I am interested in Belgium and other overseas suppliers, especially in Eastern Europe.

I would also appreciate any background, or research material, you may have concerning plastics materials most especially PVC.

Thank you for your assistance.

Yours faithfully,

(Signed)

Ton, Maxwell

Maxwell Import/Export Agency

5.3 International Trade Directories

There are a number of international trade directories available at public libraries. For example, international phone directories and world telex directories These directories have cross-referenced classifications of company names by country, by industry and alphabetically, and they give details of names, addresses, phone, fax and telex numbers, sometimes the names of the owners/directors and other useful information.

5.4 Export Contact List Service

They provide mailing prospective overseas customers mailing lists from automated commercial worldwide file of foreign firms. This list comprise of manufacturers, distributors, retailers, service firms and Government Agencies names, addresses, phone numbers, telex and names of key people, products and services. You can get this list online by searching for Commerce data.

5.5 Trade Opportunities Program

This service was designed for overseas companies interested in U.S. products and services. Details such as specifications, quality, end-use, delivery and deadlines are fed into the computer, posted on the commerce's EEB and this information is accessible to anyone with a personal computer and modem

5.6 Commercial Banks

Almost all major banks have international banking departments employing specialists conversant with specific countries and transactions. These large banks, located in most major U.S. cities, maintain offices throughout the country. Larger banks also maintain correspondent relationships with banks in most foreign countries or operate their own overseas branches, providing a direct channel to foreign customers.

Banks frequently provide assistance free of charge to their clients. Many also have publications available that discuss business practices by country and can be a valuable tool for initial familiarization with foreign industry.

Often large foreign distributors use a U.S. banks subsidiary in their country for conducting their business with the United States. In most cases, the bank will be delighted to set up an appointment between two customers. The added advantage is that payment details, should the deal be struck, are often more manageable if the bank is involved from the start. In many countries, a letter of introduction from your bank can help open doors with potential distributor candidates by establishing your company as a serious international organization. Letters of introduction have fallen out of practice, but are still useful from time to time, especially in the somewhat more formal European countries.

Banks are best at assisting with financial matters and can be of great help on a variety of services, including handling international payments, advising you on currency fluctuations and the risks to your firm, and changes in the regulatory environment in specific countries. They are also invaluable in helping you conduct credit checks on foreign firms.

5.7 International Banks

The international divisions of banks can provide a lot of useful information for both import and export agents. They produce monthly newsletters, economic surveys of countries, country profiles and, probably most important from the prospective agents point of view, lists of buyers and suppliers looking for overseas trade opportunities. The country profiles and economic surveys provide useful background information if you are interested in trade with a particular country. They tell you about the country's customs, history, trade and geography among other things. This information is often provided free of charge and you do not need to be a customer of the bank concerned. If you would like to obtain copies of these documents then you should either write to your bank or alternatively contact the international departments of the other banks.

Here is a sample letter to the bank for information

MAXWELL IMPORT & EXPORT AGENCY

8992 West 591t1 Street

Suite 001

Chicago IL 60643 U.S.A.

Phone (312) 568-8424

Fax (312) 568-8421

Norwest Bank Inc.,

International Department,

77th Street,

Chicago

For the attention of the Manager

Dear Sir,

Subject: Trade with Portugal

Will you please be kind enough to add my name to your mailing list for your international trade opportunities brochure? I am particularly interested in opportunities for trade between Portugal and United States.

Will you also please send me your latest country profile leaflet on Portugal?

Thank you for your assistance,

Yours faithfully,

(Signed)

Tom Maxwell

Maxwell Import & Export Agency

When you receive this information you should study it carefully. Usually both export and import opportunities are listed in the same publication. When you see an item which interests you mark it and then prepare a further letter to the bank requesting detailed information on this particular item. The item will have a reference number allocated to it in the publication and this should always be quoted in your letter. The bank will then forward the detailed information to you through the post so that you can contact the company concerned directly.

5.8 U.S. Department Of Commerce

The U.S. Department of Commerce has a wide array of services, at little or no cost, for assisting U.S. exporters in getting established with their international operations. These services are designed to save you time, energy, and money. The services are designed to accomplish what you want to attain with less exertion on your part and with an eye to making the process less expensive and intimidating. The goal, and the thrust of its programs, is to motivate firms that would not otherwise be able to export into the game by making the whole process easier. Please note, however, that it does charge for most services. However, for the most part, they are quite focused and knowledgeable. And with the exception of extremely costly commercially produced market research, the federal government is the only entity in the United States that is actively conducting market research abroad.

5.9 International Trade Administration

The best starting point for getting information about export programs is a district office of the International Trade Administration (ITA). Its local offices have access to all assistance available in the Department of commerce, and they can direct you to other government and private sector export services. Most of the staff in these offices have significant overseas experience and can guide you through the entire process: helping you find overseas representation, providing good information on foreign commercial laws and distribution practices, assisting you with targeting markets, checking out potential overseas representatives, and counseling you on the steps involved in exporting. You can also make use of ITA's services to assist your firm with obtaining sources for financing international deals, information on trade exhibitions answers to documentary questions, and assistance on finding your way through the export licensing procedures.

Agent Distributor Service. This customized search for interested foreign representatives will identify up to six prospects. It is an excellent way to pick up distributors, at reasonable cost, with almost no toil on your part. ITA will deliver your brochures to appropriate candidates in a country you target. Any interested candidates will get in touch with you.

Commercial News (ISA). This monthly magazine published by ITA and distributed worldwide to importers is a great way to get exposure for new product or niche products for which research and traditional targeting methods don't work well. This service is not appropriate for larger, well-recognized firms because it is a bit too broadly based for them. It works well for smaller companies, with less generous export marketing budgets.

Foreign Buyer Program. LTA promotes certain U.S. trade fairs worldwide to lure foreign buyers and importers to those fairs. Obtain a list of all of these trade fairs in your industry, and make certain that you exhibit at the fair and secure individual meetings with the foreign buyers who attend. I know of one firm that picked up seventeen distributors in fourteen countries at a single fair. As a result, the product's overseas introduction took place in a matter of weeks.

The best aspect of this service is that the foreign buyers present are normally earnest about picking up new products (hence their presence at the show), and it is a very swift process. If the foreign buyers are not interested in your products for their purposes, they can often recommend offer companies in their countries that might be interested. These foreign buyers can be invaluable sources of information and referrals because they are familiar with their market and the players.

World Traders Data Report. These custom reports, prepared by the U.S. embassy, evaluate your potential representatives or customers and include background information, standing in the local business community, creditworthiness, and overall reliability. These reports also contain useful comments" section, which has dissuaded U.S., firms from making bad decisions on a number of occasions. This section is essentially the embassy's assessment of the distributor's general operations and desirability and includes information about the candidate's best customers, what other companies he or she is active with, where branch offices are maintained, which other products he or she carries, and the like. This comments section is the meat of the report; the other information is readily available from other sources.

Overseas Trade Fairs. You should participate in one overseas trade fair early on, if for no other reason than to gain the experience of meeting new customers face to face and to learn how the competition is marketing its products. ITA makes this first effort much less difficult by providing customs clearance for your materials, turnkey booth packages, and logistical support for certain overseas fairs that it schedules annually.

5.10 Commerce Officers at U.S. Embassies Abroad

About half of the American commercial officers working in embassies have been hired directly from the private sector, and most seem to have solid international trade experience. They are backed up by a number of local employees, who are usually natives of the country and are knowledgeable about the distributors, local business law, and business practices in that country.

The commercial staff provides a range of services to help companies sell overseas:

background information on foreign companies (known as a World Trader Data Report), services designed to help you pinpoint distributors, market research, business counseling, and assistance in making appointments with key buyers and government officials. In many countries a call from the embassy will effectively pave the way for your appointment.

There are still some embassies, however, where the level of service still reflects the sort of unhelpful attitudes that we saw a decade ago. Like all other large organizations, there is some unevenness to the quality of the staff if you cannot get the sort of assistance you need from the embassy, turn to the local. U.S. chamber of commerce in that country or, as a last resort, to a business service center in a major hotel.

5.11 Country Desk Officers

These are individuals who are assigned responsibility for following all developments in a particular country that could affect U.S. business. They are an excellent source of information on trade potential in specific countries. I have found them most helpful in providing up to date information on the commercial situation in particular countries, especially those with unstable governments or economies. They also can confirm or deny information you pick up from other sources. They can educate you about a country's regulations, tariffs, business practices, economic and political developments, trade data and trends, market size and growth, and documentary requirements for that country.

Get a full listing of these officers from your local ITA district office.

5.12 Trade Development Industry Officers

These people specialize by industry sectors and closely follow business developments, worldwide, in that industry. Aside from the factual information they can provide, they are good sources of information about the general state of your industry abroad and can offer good counsel with regard to government-sponsored trade missions to foreign markets. These officers are most helpful with assisting in locating good international trade fairs, helping you stay abreast of developments overseas that could affect your business (such as emerging competitors), and providing good general information about where you might locate good markets for your products.

5.13 Industry Associations

Some U.S. industry associations can supply detailed information on market demand for their member's products in selected countries and assist members by providing information about potential distributor candidates overseas. At the very least, they can put you in touch with their counterparts in other countries; will have membership lists and newsletters to help you generate distributor leads prior to your trip. To find your association check the National Trade Association Handbook available at most libraries.

5.14 American Embassy Abroad

Another good source of information in a foreign country is the U.S. embassy. They are knowledgeable about local trade opportunities, actual and potential competition, good distributor candidates, and the like. These Embassies abroad usually field inquiries from any U.S. business but ordinarily undertake detailed service only for members of affiliated organizations. The support they offer seems to depend on the individuals running the particular office, so services vary from office to office.

5.15 Foreign Governments

Many governments conduct research on foreign market opportunities. By requesting the information through one of your foreign distributors, located in the country that has conducted the research, you can gain access to a worldwide information network. They key here is to alert all of your overseas distributors to get unto their export assistance networks and stay on the lookout for information that can help you in other markets.

5.16 Making Contact

After you have completed your contact of one or more of the above sources of information you should end up with a list of potential suppliers that you wish to turn into clients for your agency. We would say fifteen to twenty names is a good starting point. These are the names that you are going to contact and offer your services to.

They may be manufacturers, distributors, dealers or even wholesalers in the country concerned. The letter that you send for these initial contacts is very important, even though it is fairly simple. It is important that it is well-produced, typed, never hand-written, and specific.

<u>Sample contact letter to an overseas supplier</u>

MAXWELL IMPORT & EXPORT AGENCY

8992 West 89"~ Street

Suite 001

Chicago IL 60643 U.S.A.

Phone (312) 568-8421

Fax (3l2) 568-8421

22 October 2002.

Pan-Asian Supplies Ltd.,

I, Business Plaza,

Singapore

For the attention of the General Manager

Dear Sir,

Subject: Giftware

I am an import agent specializing in oriental giftware for the US market. Having seen one of your advertisements I would be very pleased to represent your interests in the US. Your excellent Product range will, without doubt, experience a ready market in this county.

If this proposal is of interest to you would you be kind enough to forward detailed brochures, price lusts for CIF Chicago (or relevant destination), payment terms applicable to orders received, and an indication of the commission rate payable to me on orders achieved.

I look forward to your reply and remain,

Yours faithfully,

(Signed)

Tom Maxwell

Maxwell Import & Export Agency.

5.16.1 Notes on Writing a Business Letter

   (a)   Make sure you always state your full name, address, country and phone or fax number.

   (b)   Always try to address your letters to a person if possible; if you don't have a name then address it to the General Manager.

(c)   Always give the letter a heading, in this case: Giftware.

(d)   Always ask for the payment terms applicable to orders received

(e)   Never state the commission you want in initial contact letters let them make the offer -it might be more than you were going to ask, and if it isn't then you can negotiate with them in the follow-up letter.

(f)   Always sign your letters and make sure your name is typed underneath in case your signature is illegible. Include a business title such as Managing Director, General Manager, International Trade Consultant or similar. A business name follows the title.

(g)   Remember that a letter is an advertisement for your business. In fact it will be the first chance for a prospective supplier to gain an impression of your agency.

5.17 Your First Contract

We have discussed above the initial contact letters that you will send; now we will look at how that process will develop. Your first contact will probably be in the form of a letter responding to your correspondence. This reply may take some time in arriving; three to four weeks is not unusual so don't worry if it takes a while. The first reply you receive, especially if it arrives in an airmail envelope covered with exotic stamps, is in itself an exciting experience! Up until that point it's all been theory - now it all starts to come together and happen. Also check your E-mail as well as your fax if you have one.

If you are dealing with an English-speaking country, then you will have no problems with understanding the reply. In fact, most countries either have English as their second language or use it for commercial purposes. For example, all the correspondence we have ever seen from countries as diverse as Poland, Brazil, India and Taiwan has been in

English. However, some replies may not be in English. Here are some services that might help.

5.17.1 Translations

You may need to translate your letter into other languages. One of the best, cheapest, and most user-friendly services available is the Massachusetts-based WordNet. It accepts documents for translation via fax at any time and passes them onto one of the 400 translators who freelance for comparatively reasonable fee. WordNet will also review the quality of the translation if the topic is sufficiently complicated.

Prices vary, but most translations cost $25 to $50 per IOU words, and WordNet will typeset and print the documents as well. Technical and difficult language translations will be extra. Contact WordNet at (508) 264-0600.

Several commercially developed software programs automatically translate in and out of English from several European languages. However, these programs are not sufficiently well developed yet for good business usage. An added problem is that most of these programs are currently available only in European languages.

5.17.2 Videoconferencing

Buying videoconferencing equipment may be a sizable initial investment. AT&T. MCI new offers its Mail Global Access.

5.17.3 Interpreters

AT&T offers a service that allows you to speak, via an interpreter from AT&T (and with a toll-free line if you choose), to other businesspeople around the world. Because of time differences, this service is available twenty-four hours a day, and AT&T has the ability to deliver over 140 languages to you instantly. The service is not cheap, but is not out of line for the value offered.

Generally speaking, the replies you receive will be of a positive nature and this is in itself encouraging when you are starting out in a business venture. There are a number of crucial things to look for in these initial letters. Watch for the following points:

(a) Have they accepted your offer of an agency?

(b) If so, at what commission rate?

(c) Have they enclosed the brochures that you need?

(d) What currency have they quoted in? Often Far Eastern suppliers will quote in US Dollars, but don't worry about that as we will cover it in a later chapter.

(e) Have they indicated the payment terms applicable to orders that you achieve on their behalf'?

(f) Are there any other matters covered in the letter?

5.18 Your Response

Let us consider your response to this letter and others you will receive from potential suppliers. If you get several letters offering you agencies all for the same Product range? You can accept all the offers and try to achieve sales for all the suppliers but that could prove confusing. It is usually better to accept the one that either

(a) Offers you the greater commission rate

(b) Appear to have the better quality of product.

(c) Has the most competitive pricing, or

(d) Has the least distance to ship

If you are going to accept the offer of a supplier and become his agent, then you will need to check the items listed in the section above before sending your confirmation. This confirmation should indicate your acceptance of the offer subject to seeing the full agency agreement. In fact this may never be forthcoming; the agency can rest on the basis of your correspondence and that of your client.

If you are clear on the points listed above then you have a good picture of what you are taking on. If there are points in your supplier's letter that you are unhappy about, for example the commission rate, then you should reply immediately indicating clearly what the problem is. Until you get these issues resolved you should not take any action concerning the agency; do not, for example, do any promotional work for the supplier or send out any quotations to potential buyers as this could imply that you have accepted the agency on the original terms. Wait for a satisfactory solution to your request first.

Sample follow-up letter to an international supplier

MAXWELL IMPORT & EXPORT AGENCY

8992 West 89"' Street

Suite #201

Chicago IL 60643 U.S.A.

Phone (312) 568-8421

Fax (312) 568-8421

IC November 1997

Pan-Asian Supplies Ltd,

I Business Plan,

Singapore 10

For the attention of the General Manager

Dear Sir,

Thank you for your letter of 27th October 2002. I was very pleased to read that you wish to appoint me as your representative in Midwest United states for your range of giftware. Before we discuss the detail of the agreement can you please clarify two points for me?

Firstly, you do not indicate in your letter the commission rate payable to me for orders obtained. Can you please confirm this rate?

Secondly, can you please clarify the payment terms required from buyers in Midwest region, United States? I look forward to receiving this information. As soon as these matters are resolved I will confirm my acceptance of the agency and we can commence work.

Yours faithfully,

(Signed)

Tom Maxwell

General Manager

When you have a positive confirmation from the supplier this means you have now been appointed as an import commission agent and your business has really begun.

5.19 What You Can Expect

You can expect the following from your client

1.   Your Commission

This is payable once your supplier has received his payment from the buyer. It is rare to experience difficulty obtaining your commission as the supplier will be eager to retain you

2. Information

- Regular information on the progress of orders you have obtained for him. This would cover such things as the value of the order, the scheduled shipping date, the payment terms or any changes in the order.

- Regular information concerning his Products. For example, details of new Products available, price changes, and specification changes, technical innovations, advertising campaigns and sales initiatives.

.3.   Promotional Material

This includes brochures, leaflets, notices, give aways and samples. You usually get an initial supply free of charge and then may need to pay for further supplies. You probably think that it would be in the supplier's interests to give you as much of this material free of charge as possible. Unfortunately this is not always so. Try to reach an understanding with your client from the beginning concerning such materials, for instance that you receive a minimum, guaranteed quantity over a period free of charge. If you have materials produced locally yourself try to obtain some assistance with the costs from your client.

4.   Good Product Support

A good working relationship with the supplier will lead to a successful business for both parties. An essential part of thus relationship is good technical support from the client for his Products and, if possible, training about the use of the Products.

5.20 What the Supplier will Expect

You do need to know also what the supplier (your client) will expect from you in return for your commission.

1.   Obtaining orders

You will be expected to obtain orders for his Products. He will probably expect you to sell them at the price given in his price list, although sometimes this is left to the discretion of the agent providing a minimum price is maintained. You may need to add freight, insurance and importation charges to this price if the client has only quoted FOB.

2. Promoting the Product

You may be expected to promote his Products. This means getting his Products known in the market place by mail-shots and other promotional activity. This is not always a condition of the agency but you need to be aware of it. Often your client will provide the promotional literature required in the form of brochures, samples and price lists. In some cases, however, you may be expected to provide this literature yourself Try to avoid this at first as advertising material can be expensive to produce.

3. Preparing a market report

You may be expected to provide a market research report for him. This report would detail

(a) The size of the market.

(b) The major competitors for the business.

(c) The usual selling price for the Product. If it is a consumer Product then this is fairly easy as you can go into a shop and find out, if it is an industrial Product then you can send for catalogues and price lists of competitive Products on sale in the market.

(d) The methods used for selling the Product. Is it sold mainly by mail order, through department stores, direct from a distributor or a combination of several different outlets?

(e) The way you intend to sell his Products.

Assistance in preparing such a report is given in Chapters 4 and 8.

5. Mediation

You will be expected to act as an intermediary between your client and the buyer. You will relay messages, possibly negotiate sales contracts between buyer and supplier, oversee delivery, and perhaps assist in the shipping arrangements for the goods. Usually, however, the agent's involvement once the contract between buyer and seller has been agreed is minimal, the main parties then preferring to deal direct. This is no way jeopardizes your commission which will still be paid in full when the supplier receives his payment from the buyer.

4. Progress reports

You may be expected to provide progress reports. These reports are usually prepared on an annual (or monthly) basis, the purpose of them being to keep the supplier informed of your progress in the market and your expectations for the near future. They would include such information as sales achieved by units and revenue, promotional activity carried out and planned, potential orders awaited or state of the market, indeed anything relevant for your client. There is rarely a laid down format for these reports so invent your own layout ensuring that it is type-written and well presented. A sample report is given below.

Sample monthly' agent's reports

MAXWELL IMPORT & EXPORT AGENCY

8992 West 89" Street

Suite 001

Chicago IL 60643 U.S.A.

Phone (312) 568-8421

Fax (312) 568-8421

TOM MAXWELL, ACTING ON BEHALF OF: HONG KONG TOY CORPORATION

SALES AND MARKETING REPORT FOR MAY, 2002

(A)   SALES Z4CIIJE FED:

Note: Y-T-D = Year to Date (All figures are in U.S. Dollars)

PRODUCT	MONTH UNITS	MONTH REV $	Y-T-[] UNITS	Y-T-[] REVS
Comp Games	17,500	122,500	61,000	427,000

Puzzles	9,060	3,620	29,000	43,500
Toy Cars	1,120	30,240	3,100	83,700
Dolls	110,220	62,670	260,400	195,300
Total	137,920	249,030	353,500	749,500

(B)   FORECAST UNITS & REVENUE JUNE - NOVEMBER 1997

PRODUCT	6 MONTH UNITS	6 MONTH REV $	Y-T-D UNITS	Y-T-D REVS
Comp Games	73,200	512,400	134,200	939,400
Puzzles	34,600	52,200	63,800	95,700
Toy Cars	3,720	100,440	6,820	184,140
Dolls	312,480	234,360	572,880	429,660
Total	424,200	899,400	777,700	1,648,900

(C)   MMOR CUSTOMERS

Trick stores (Retail) Inc, Chicago

TBC Toy Company, Indianapolis

A&C Toys (Wholesale) Inc., Gary

(D)   COMMISSION ACCOUNT - 2002

Commission earned Ian - May 2002	$37,470.50
Forecast commission Jun. - Nov. 2002	$44,970.00
Total	$8244050

(E)   MARKETING PLANS

   1) Launch of new spacemen Products - July 1997

   2) Direct mailing to retailers/wholesalers - Aug/Sep. 1Q97

   3) Attend Toy Fair In St Louis - Oct. 1997

(F)   COMMENTARY

The United States market is expected to grow by 8.7 per cent during 1997. Our research through various government statistics indicates that most of this growth will be achieved by imported Products. We would appreciate your confirmation of the following points:

   (a) That we have exclusive selling rights of the 'spacemen range in United States.

   (b) Our commission rate on these new products will increase to 12 per cent.

END OF REPORT

5.21 Visiting Your Client

As you prove yourself successful to your client the relationship will grow and the business will expand. There comes a point where either the client will want to visit you, or he will want you to visit him. This face-to-face contact is an essential part of the growth process in an agency relationship.

This meeting is of the utmost importance. If you are visiting your client then make sure that you make the travel arrangements in plenty of time and that you have an itinerary worked out beforehand. Careful planning must be made for this visit to be successful. Make sure that you have read about the country concerned and you know something of the people and their culture and customs. Check to see if entry visas are required. You may also need inoculation certificates if you are visiting certain countries - check with your local travel agent to make sure.

If the client is visiting you then make sure that you plan for this as carefully as you would plan a visit to him. Offer to help with his hotel and travel arrangements (not financially) assist him in making appointments with potential and current buyers. It often helps with your selling if your customers meet and talk with the overseas supplier; it will in no way jeopardize your commission but could prove very beneficial to the business. Generally make his visit pleasant and constructive. Note that in most cases the cost of these visits is borne by the client whether the visit is made by you or him. Make sure that this is understood from the outset,

The purpose of such visits is two-fold:

(a) To either give you a feel for the clients business, possibly involving Product training and induction training, or to give the client a feel for the market if he is visiting you.

(b) To discuss and put into action specific programs for maintaining and expanding the business. This could involve customer visits, promotion campaigns, trade shows, and exhibitions and so on. This face-to-face contact really can cement the relationship and drive the business forward.

5.22 Getting Started

Let us now proceed with the specific Issues involved in becoming an export commission agent.

Instead of representing the interests of an overseas supplier, as is the case with an import commission agent, the export agent represents the interests of a US manufacturer or supplier. Once again you can act on behalf of more than one client. What you are seeking to achieve is sales of a home Product or service in an overseas market. For accomplishing this you receive a commission, normally expressed as a percentage of the order value.

You can achieve this objective in one of two ways.

(a) You can find international buyers who are seeking specific goods and match their requirements with a US producer of the goods.

(b) You can find US suppliers who are looking for export markets for their goods or services and match their requirements with overseas buyers of the goods.

In either case the US supplier will be the client and you will receive your commission from the client on completion of the order.

5.23 Making Contact

In selecting the names to contact it can prove useful to first try those that are in the same geographic area as yourself for the sake of convenience.

When you have completed your contact of the above sources of information you should end up with a list of potential suppliers that you wish to turn into clients for your export agency. We would recommend fifteen to twenty names as a good starting point. These are the names that you are going to contact and offer your services to. The letter that you send for these initial contacts is going to be very important. It is important that it is well produced, typed, never hand-written, and specific.

<u>Sample contact letter to a potential supplier</u>

MAXWELL IMPORT & EXPORT AGENCY

8992 West 39th Street

Suite #001

Chicago IL 60643, U.S.A.

Phone (312) 568-8421

Fax (312) 568-3421

28 October 2003

A T C Suppliers Inc.,

38th Street, Unit 1,

Gainesville,

FL 32609

<u>For the attention of Mr. Jones. Commercial Director</u>

Dear Mr. Jones,

Subject: Export of Industrial Tools

I see in this month's copy of the Overseas Trade Bulletin that you are seeking export opportunities for your range of industrial tools. I am an export agent with contacts in Australia and Norway who have expressed interest in importing such industrial tools.

Would you please be kind enough to forward descriptive literature for all of your Products, including FOB Chicago prices? I would like to forward copies of these to my contacts. Fifteen copies would be sufficient at this stage.

In the event of my achieving a successful order for your company I would request the payment of a commission (please indicate the level of commission that you would be prepared to offer) expressed as a percentage of the FOB value of the order. Please confirm that this is acceptable to you.

I look forward to receiving the required literature and thank you for your assistance.

Yours sincerely,
(Signed)
Tom Maxwell
Maxwell Import & Export Agency

5.24 Notes on Writing Business Letters

(a) Always try to address correspondence, whether it is letter, fax or telex, to a named person rather than just the company concerned. This increases the chance of your letter actually getting read and dealt with. You can easily find out the name of the relevant person to whom to send the letter by phoning the company and asking them.

(b) Keep the letter brief and other point at this stage and always include a heading, in this case 'Export of Industrial Tools'.

(c) If you do not have specific areas in mind for your agency activity (in the above example we have used Australia and Norway), then simply ask which areas the company currently has available for new agents.

(d) Remember that the letter is an advertisement for your business, in That it is the first thing that they will see concerning you and your business.

(e) It is also useful to enclose one of your business cards, if you have any, with the letter. This will probably be kept by the recipient for future reference.

(f) For further details of FOB (Free on Board) and other delivery terms

'Cold-calling'

This term simply means making contact with a company or individual who you do not know and have had no previous contact with; it usually involves sending an initial contact letter and following upon this with either a second letter or phone call. It can be particularly useful where you do not know if the potential supplier is currently exporting or not.

However, many people have a great fear' of cold calling - usually because they have a misconception of what is involved. It is in fact a very effective method of generating sales. To assist you in this important task let us give you a few guidelines:

*   Preparation

It is critically important that you have adequately prepared yourself for a cold-calling session. You should have a list of the people who you are going to speak to with their phone numbers. Have a blank sheet of paper or notebook ready for any notes you may need to take.

*   Attitude

You must have the right attitude to cold-calling. If you view it as a necessary and useful part of your business you will stop seeing it as a problem.

*   Timing

The timing of your letter or call can make a considerable difference to whether or not it is successful. Good times to contact are during the first working hour of each day, immediately after lunch and during the last working hour of the day. Avoid, if possible, Monday mornings, Friday afternoons and lunch times.

*   Content

Use a script. Carefully write down what you are going to say before you start the session. This is another important part of your preparation If you work with a script you will avoid making mistakes, losing your words or repeating yourself Practice your script before writing your letter or making your call - after a while it will become so familiar to you that it will sound quite natural.

A good script should contain the following:
- Greeting: Good morning/afternoon etc
- Introduction: I am Tom Maxwell from -Maxwell import & export Agency
- Purpose: I would like to talk to you about
- Objective: I would like to arrange an appointment with you
- Close: It was a pleasure speaking to you
- Follow-up

You must follow up a successful letter or call immediately. For example, if you have arranged an appointment, write to confirm it. If the person wants further information, send it that day. There is no point in going to all the trouble of making the contact if you do nothing with the result of those calls.

If you follow these simple steps then cold-calling will hold no fear for you.

5.25 Notes on Sample 'Cold-Calling Letter'

- We have assumed that you do not have a contact name for this letter. If you have one then so much the better.

- This letter should be followed up about 7 to 10 days later by a further letter or with a phone call, providing of course that you haven't received a reply in the meantime. The aim is to find out if the letter was received and if so to whom it has been passed and what action is likely to be taken upon it.

- The suggestion of a meeting should only be made if you are willing to invest the money in traveling to their location. Face-to-face meetings are useful because they help to build the relationship.

- If you have any, enclose one of your business cards with the letter.

Sample Cold- calling letter

MAXWELL IMPORT & EXPORT AGENCY

8992 West 39th Street

Suite 001

Chicago IL 60643, U.S.A.

Phone (312) 568-8421

Fax (3l2) 568-8421

28 October 2002

A.T.C. Suppliers Inc.,

38th Street, Unit I,

Gainesville, FL 32609

For the attention of the Vice President

Dear Sir,

Subject: Export of Industrial Tools

I am an export agent seeking to explore several export markets on behalf of U.S manufacturers of quality industrial Products. I know of your Products and their excellent reputation for quality. I would very much like to discuss with you opportunities for exporting your Products.

To give me some further background information before our meeting perhaps you would be kind enough to send me copies of your brochures and related literature including your standard price list. I would also be grateful if you would indicate those export markets, if any, to which you are currently shipping.

I look forward to your reply and to meeting with you in The near future.

Yours faithfully, (Signed)

Tom Maxwell

General Manager

Maxwell Import & Export Agency

Although the replies you receive will normally be of a positive nature, suppliers in US is more likely to want to discuss The matter further before committing Themselves to an agency agreement with you. This may be by correspondence or by face-to-face meeting at their company.

The points you should watch for in these replies to your initial contact letters are as follows.

(a) Have they accepted your offer of an agency? Have they requested a meeting, or do they want further details first? (For example, do they want more information about you or how you intend to tackle marketing their Products?)

(b) Have they indicated a commission rate?

(c) Have they enclosed the literature that you requested?

(d) Have they provided the price lists that you requested?

(e) Have they indicated the payment terms applicable to orders that you achieve on their behalf? (For instance how will the buyer have to pay for the goods?)

(f) Are there any other matters covered in the letter? For example, would you be interested in an agency in a different region or for different Products?

5.26 What Now?

If the reply to your request has been positive and the supplier has agreed your offer of an agency than you will now need to make the decision as to whether or not you are going to accept him as your client. If you have all the information that you need then you will have a good picture of what you are taking on. On the other hand, before agreeing to the agency, you need to know what the client will expect from you.

- Orders for his Products from the markets you have been assigned.
- You may be expected to promote his Products. This means getting the Products known in the market place by mail-shots and other promotional activity.
- You may be expected to provide progress reports at agreed intervals, for instance once a year, a simple example of which is given below.
- You will be expected to act as an intermediary between your client and the buyer.
- You will relay messages, negotiate orders between buyer and seller, oversee delivery and possibly assist in the shipping arrangements for the goods. Usually, however, your involvement once the order between buyer and supplier has been agreed is minimal.

If there are other questions on any of these matters you should write back to the company detailing the questions you have. Hopefully these matters will either not arise or will be quickly clarified by the supplier. If, however, you are unhappy with the answers or feel that you are, withdraw from the discussions - there will be plenty of good opportunities so don't just take anything that is offered to you.

5.27 What You can Expect

In the main you can expect to receive the same items as an export agent as you would as an import agent, that is.

- Your commission
- Regular information on the progress of orders
- Product information
- Advertising material

- Possibly sample Products and Product training

This last item is likely to take on more importance when you are acting as the agent for a local company. Because you are resident in the same country as your client he is in a much better position to train you and to support you.

5.28 What the Client will Expect

Progress reports

You may be expected to provide regular progress reports. These reports are usually prepared annually and sometimes monthly or quarterly, the purpose of them being to keep the client informed of your progress in the market and your expectations for the near future. They would include such information as sales achieved by units and revenue, promotional activity carried out and planned, potential orders awaited or state of the market, indeed anything relevant for your client. There is rarely a laid down format for these reports so invent your own layout ensuring that it is type-written and well presented. An example, standard monthly agent's report is given below.

5.29 Meetings with Clients

As an export agent you are likely to have meetings with your client(s) at times, perhaps regularly. This is probably going to involve you visiting the location of the client rather than him visiting you. In fact, because of your both being it, the same country it is likely that the relationship in general will be much closer than with import agency. There will be greater Product and literature support and probably some Product training.

This is to be welcomed and you should have no concerns over these meetings even if you have only a small agency business. Everyone has to start somewhere and providing you give a good service nobody is likely to mind that you haven't a huge business structure behind you. However, it is important that you approach these meetings with both forward-planning and confidence. These two factors are equally important for a successful meeting. The planning involves preparing notes for the meeting covering what you intend doing for your client (for instance facts or forecasts on potential markets and sales opportunities), and the questions you need to ask the client. The confidence is essential because you can achieve nearly anything by being confident. It means being relaxed, sure of your information and demonstrating to the supplier that you are determined to succeed both for him and for you. This confidence can be learned like anything else and comes from having a positive attitude to your occupation. You will succeed if you believe you can succeed.

Sample monthly export agents report

MAXWELL IMPORT & EXPORT AGENCY

8992 West 89'" Street

Suite 001

Chicago IL 60642, U.S.A.

Phone (312) 568-8421

Fax (312) 568-8421

Tom Maxwell (EXPORT) AGENCY ACTING ON BEHALF OF A.T.C. SUPPLIER Note Y-T-D = Year to date

SALES AND MARKETING REPORT FOR MAY 2002

(A)   SALES ACHIEVED:

(All figures are in U.S. $)

PRODUCT	MONTH UNITS	MONTH REVENUE	Y-T-D UNITS
AUSTRALIAN MARKET			
Hand tools	1250	31250	4250
Welding Tools	250	43750	800
Calibration equip.	50	27500	120
TOTAL	1550	102500	5170
NORWEGIAN MARKET			
Hand tools	250	6250	1150
Welding Tools	150	3750	350
Calibration equipment	30750	110	
TOTAL	430	10750	1610
GRAND TOTAL	1080	113250	6780

(B) FORECAST UNITS & REVENUE JUNE - NOVEMBER 2002

(All figures are in U.S. Dollars)

PRODUCT	6 MONTH UNITS	6 MONTH REVENUE	Y-T-D UNITS
AUSTRALIAN MARKET			
Hand Tools	5500	137500	9750
Welding Tools	1200	210000	2000

Calibration Equipment	150	82500	270
TOTAL	6850	430000	12020
NORWEGIAN MARKET			
Hand tools	1250	31250	2400
Welding Tools	500	12500	850
Calibration Equip.	150	3750	260
TOTAL	1900	47500	3510
TOTAL	8750	477500	15530

(C) MAJOR CUSTOMERS

Genesee Precision Industries Ltd., Perth Long tools Ventures Ltd., Oslo 53

(D)   COMMISSION ACCOUNT

Commission earned Jan - May 2002	$17,620
Forecast commission June - November 2002	$23,870
Total	$41,500

(E)   MARKETING PLANS

(a) Mail-shot 175 Norwegian wholesale outlets - August 2002

(b) Advertise in trade magazine in Australia - November 2002

END OF REPORT

6.0 The Agency Agreement

6.1 Agency Appointment

There does not have to be a written agency agreement for an agent to be appointed. Often agencies are created verbally, or are implied in letters, faxes, telexes or other correspondence between client and agent. Some exist by virtue of the fact that the two parties are doing business with each other in a particular way, even in rare cases without either party being aware that it is an agency agreement!

So that you are sure about this important point we will show below how agency agreements come about, both verbal agreements and written ones. You should never be in doubt on this issue - you have either clearly been appointed as an agent or you have not.

6.2 Verbal Agency Agreement

Many agencies are written in nature or a mixture of verbal and written. This mixture can occur when parts of the agreement are included in letters between the parties, and parts are only passed by word of mouth between the parties. These verbal agreements are just as binding and have much the same implications for both parties as a more formal, written agency agreement signed by both parties.

A verbal agreement exists when you are informed that you can proceed with obtaining orders and can act on behalf of another party. From that point onwards both parties are bound by an implied agency agreement until the relationship ends. It is often easier to terminate such an agreement and there are not as many potential conditions attached to the agency. Verbal agreements are especially useful when the client-agent relationship exists for one transaction only.

Some clients will not consider a written agreement until the relationship has passed through a trial period when both parties can judge the merits of the system. They will want to make sure that you can promote their Products before committing themselves to a fixed agreement.

It is possible to have a perfectly valid oral contract. Reducing a contract to writing is not a prerequisite to its enforceability. The exception to that general rule is found within the Statute of Frauds. The Statute of Frauds is a collective term describing the various statutory provisions which render unenforceable certain types of contracts unless they are evidenced by writing. The Statute of Frauds does not mean that oral agreements within the scope of the Statute cannot be made and performed or that they are illegal. It merely means that enforcement may be unavailable if one of the parties refuses to fulfill their obligations.

6.3 Written Agency Agreements

Written agreements are more common than verbal agreements. Note that the term written agreement covers both formal, specific agency agreement documents and informal, general correspondence that creates a client-agent relationship. More often than not your appointment will be in the form of a letter from the client. "Signature" merely means any authentication which identifies the party to be charged in a law suit if one party does not perform. Even a letterhead or an "X" will do, provided it is placed on the writing with the intent to authenticate it. To assist you we have given later examples of both formal and informal agency agreements.

6.4 Factors Influencing Written Agency Agreements

The agency agreement can take a number of different forms depending upon several factors that we will discuss below. These are:

- The county of residence of the client

- The nature of the agency

- The nature of the product, or industry

- The degree of association between the client and the agent

Note that the term written agreement covers both formal, specific agency agreement documents and informal, general correspondence that creates a client-agent relationship. More often than not your appointment will be in the form of a letter from the client.

Country of the Client

The wording of; and the conditions of; the agreement may vary depending upon the country of residence of the client. By and large the agreement will be determined by the client. Admittedly this will involve a discussion with the agent before the agreement is drawn up, but it still remains true that the client is the one who offers the agreement to the agent. Because of this and because each country has its own interpretation of agency law, you will find that agreements vary from country to country. However, you should always find certain basic features that are common to all agreements irrespective of the county concerned.

If at all possible arrange for the agreement to be subject to the law of the country where you reside. If; however, your client will not accept this condition but instead insists on the agreement being subject to the law of his country do not worry about it - agency agreements are rarely the cause of legal dispute. All agency agreements, like any business relationship, are based upon a degree of trust which is essential for international trade to take place at all.

Nature of the Agency

The agreement will also vary depending upon the nature of the agency. For example, an agreement for an agent providing after-sales service to the buyers would differ from one where the agent merely obtains orders for his Clients goods. Similarly, the agreement for an agent holding stocks on consignment (see later section) would differ. The appointment of a distributor would certainly require a written agreement. The more complex the relationship the more complex the agreement.

Nature of the Product

A written agreement will also vary with the Product or industry involved. For example, if you are an agent for computer Products then the agreement is likely to cover, in addition to the basics common to all agreements, such things as after-sales service, warranties and spares. Whereas none of this would be necessary if you are an agent for china ornaments. However, all of these additional services can be arranged through third-party service contractors or agencies.

Degree of Association

This means the closeness of the relationship between client and agent. If you are going to act purely as a commission agent with no involvement with your client beyond obtaining orders then this will require a much simpler agreement than if you are going to carry out joint marketing activity and special joint promotions such as trade shows, or, in some cases, even have common directors of the two companies.

6.5 Implied Agency

Both verbal and written agency agreements are what are termed 'express' agencies. This has nothing to do with speed, but means that these agencies are accepted by both parties and are obvious to any outside observer, implied agency is not so obvious. This actually occurs far more frequently than people think. If a friend mentions that he has a car for sale and you in turn have another friend who is looking for a secondhand car, then by introducing the two and taking, say 10 per cent, of the cost of the car as your 'cut' for the introduction you are actually creating an agency arrangement, simple though it may be. This happens in the wider scale of business all the time with people hardly aware that they are acting as agents.

Take a simple example in the international trade arena. If you see a company advertising for supplies of a Product, for example security equipment, and know of an overseas supplier then you may put the buyer in touch with that supplier requesting as per cent commission. By implication you are now the agent of that supplier whether you, or the supplier, realize it or not.

"Because formalities are not required to create an agency relationship, one can be implied from the conduct of the parties toward each other, regardless of each party's intent, or label used to describe their relationship. The conduct of each party can create an agency relationship even if each has signed an acknowledgment for denying the existence of such a relationship. Thus, agency relationships can result unintentionally, accidentally, or inadvertently."

"An implied agency relationship is dangerous when created as the duties and obligations of agency arise -- usually without the agent's knowledge.

6.6 Termination and Renewal of Agency Agreements

Termination of Agency:

There are two methods of terminating the agent-client relationship

(a) Action of the Parties

The action of the parties can terminate an agency agreement, for instance if both parties agree to end the agreement. However, both panics have to agree to this - it cannot be decided by one party alone. The purpose of an agency agreement is to create a specific relationship that continues until the agreement is mutually terminated. This must be borne in mind when you accept the offer of an agency.

(b) Expiry of the Agreement

Of course, if the agreement is for a specific period of time, the termination may take the form of letting the agency lapse instead of renewing it. Agreements can be for either a fixed duration or an indefinite period.

Renewal of agency:

A brief word about the renewal of agency agreements. Many agreements are drawn up for a specific period of time, for instance 12 months. At, or near, the end of this period both parties will assess the value of the agreement over the previous period to see if it is worth continuing the relationship. If it is worthwhile then the current agreement may be extended for a further period or a new agreement drawn up. This gives both parties the opportunity to re-negotiate the terms of the agreement, for example you may ask for a higher rate of commission owing to your success over the previous period. Alternatively, the client may request that some sales targets are inserted into the new agreement.

Renewal is generally a fairly smooth process, especially if the agency has proved successful.

6.7 Rights of the Agent

There are a number of rights attaching to the agent m an agency agreement

(a) Commission

The agent has the right to his agreed commission. This commission should be paid in accordance with the terms of the agreement, for instance eight per cent of the value of the goods payable on completion of the order. Normally the commission is notified to the agent by credit note with actual payment following at the end of the month. Sometimes you may be required to invoice the client for the commission.

(b) Expenses

The agent is entitled to the payment of expenses incurred carrying out the express (written) wishes of the client. That means that if the client tells you to take out magazine advertising for his Products then he must be prepared to reimburse you for the cost incurred. However, if you decide on your own account to do such advertising then you may not be entitled to payment for it. It is usual to reclaim these expenses after they have been incurred by submitting a copy of the invoice or receipt, evidencing the expenses and that they have been paid by the agent if it is going to be a major item of expenditure then you can ask the client for an advance against an estimate of the cost involved.

(c) Sole agency status

If the agent has been granted a sole agency for the territory concerned, the client cannot introduce a further agent for the same goods. Territory, when applied to an export agent, usually refers to a specific country, for instance Germany. In some cases it may be more closely defined, such as the Mid-West of the United States. If the agency is proving particularly successful in one country then you may ask the client to extend the agreement to cover other related territories. In the case of an import agent, often a sole agency agreement will be given where the whole of the country is covered. In some cases the territory may be more closely defined and certain counties or regions maybe allocated.

Normally, the agent requests a particular territory rather than the client offering a territory.

(d) Information
The agent is entitled to fill information concerning the status of any orders obtained by him, for instance delivery dates or delays.

(e) Change of terms
Any changes to the agency agreement must be agreed by both parties, preferably in writing. There is no need for a new agreement to be drawn up; an existing agreement can be changed.

(f) Liability
Lastly, the agent is not liable under the contract for payment for the goods; you bear no financial risk.

6.8 Your Commission

This is of crucial importance to your business; it is after all what you are in business for. What commission rate will you be paid? How will this be paid? How do you make sure that you do get paid? Let us examine these questions:

6.8.1 Commission Rate

Usually the supplier will offer you a rate of commission at the time of your appointment as his agent. It is best to wait and see what is being offered before requesting a specific commission rate. In this way you may just be offered more than you expected. If the rate is acceptable to you then no other action is required. However, if the rate is too low then you should immediately request a revised rate before you start doing business. Commission rates will vary depending upon the industry, nature of the agreement, profit margin of the client and level of sales achieved by the agent. The rate may even vary from order to order, each case being treated individually. As a very general rule of thumb between 5 and 25 per cent is the norm.

6.8.2 Factors Influencing Commission Rates

(a) The Industry

For example, in the engineering industry 5 per cent is a common commission rate. In contrast, with some consumer goods and leisure Products the rate can go up as high as 20 per cent.

(b) Nature of the Agreement

For example, if it is an agency where after-sales service is provided by the agent the commission rate increases by quite a few percentage points. (This service can be sub-contracted by the agent to a local company.)

(c) Level of Sales Achieved by the Agent

If you are producing a good volume of sales then your commission rate may be increased as a reward for your effort, for instance from 7 to 9 per cent.

(d) Profit Margin of the Client

If the client is forced to sell at a low profit margin, perhaps because the market is very competitive, then the agent's commission rate will be limited and in some instances less than five per cent could be offered. This low rate can still prove very profitable for you as it is often compensated by the high value and size of the average transaction.

6.9 Payment of Commission

Commission can be paid in a number of ways.

- By bank transfer directly to your account in whichever currency you require is probably the simplest method.

- By international check (bank draft) to you personally at your address.

- In the currency of the order to your overseas bank account. This can be useful if you do not want to bring the funds into the country.

From the point of view of the agent, all of these methods are quite acceptable as they do not involve either cost or risk for the agent. You will normally receive your fill commission as soon as your client receives his payment from the buyer. If 'Letter of Credit' or 'Bill of Exchange is involved your commission will be paid almost immediately. You will either be paid in the currency of the order or you may receive the amount converted to your country's currency.

Extended terms are usually only applicable to capital goods contracts, which are major industrial goods such as locomotives or furnaces. If the order is subject to extended payment terms (for instance in excess of six months), try to negotiate a part-settlement (for instance 50 per cent) at the time of shipment.

Negotiating a Higher Commission Rate.

If you prove yourself a successful agent for the client then you can try to negotiate a more favorable commission rate. Either you can ask for a higher fixed rate, for instance from 7 to 9 per cent; or you can have a scale of commission rates dependent upon the size of the order. For example 7 per cent on all orders below $5000 and 8.5 per cent on all orders above that figures. Commission rates may be determined in the original agency agreement but even so they may be re-negotiated at any time,

Alternatively ask for an over-achievement bonus. For example, if you have agreed on total sales for the current year of $45,000 at a commission rate of S per cent then try to negotiate a deal whereby any sales in excess of that figure after a commission rate of 10 per cent.

6.9.1 Responsibilities of the Agent

As well as having rights under the agency agreement, the agent also has some responsibilities to his client. For example:

- You cannot sell goods at a price other than that laid down by the client without the specific written authority of the client.
- To act in good faith, for instance not to sell goods that have been provided as samples only, not to sell confidential information concerning the client's business.

Basically not to do anything that would damage the business of the client,

- To act personally and not to sub-contract the work of the agency to others unless they are employees, sub-agents or are associates of your company. (Although if after-sales service is required for the Product then this can be sub-contracted to an outside company.)

Generally speaking these are simple, common-sense issues. Although an agent has no liability on a contract of sale (that rests with the client), there can be exceptions to this general rule. For example, suppose a buyer is not informed that you are the agent and he then contracts to purchase goods from you. You pass the order back to your client. If the goods are not supplied for whatever reason and the buyer complains to you for breach of contract, you cannot at that stage say you are just the agent. It is too late as you have led the buyer to believe that you are the principal to the contract.

So, make it clear to potential customers from your first contact letter that you are acting as an export, or import, agent, not as the supplier.

6.10 Authority of the Agent

The agent has three degrees of authority.

1.   Express

He has express authority; this means the specific authority given to him under the agency agreement. For example, the agreement will state exactly what goods the agent can sell and where.

2.   Implied

He has implied authority to perform tasks that are a reasonable part of his agency business.

For example, promoting his client's goods, negotiating with buyers on contractual issues, for instance delivery method, shipment dates, and documentation requirements.

3.   Usual

He has usual authority, which means that he can carry out tasks that are 'usual' for that profession. For example, it is usual for agents to discuss delivery terms with potential clients even if not stated in the agency agreement.

The agreement itself will detail the express authority you have, for example whether you can accept customer orders or whether you have to refer them back to the client for acceptance; whether you are allowed to negotiate on price and so on.

Let us look at a simple agency agreement document to see how this relates to the conditions outlined above.

SAMPLE AGENCY AGREEMENT

This is an agreement between A.T.C. Supplier Inc.., 38~ Street, Unit I, Gainesville FL 32609 (the Principal), and Tom Maxwell, 8992 West 38th Street, Suite 001, Chicago IL 60643 (the Agent).

Dated this 15th day of November, 2002. It is hereby agreed that:

(1) The Client appoints the Agent as Sole Agent in the territory of Spain for the period of one year. The agreement to be reviewed at that time and renewed for a further period of one year if both parties agree.

(2) The Products covered by this agreement are: Industrial Tools and Instruments, and any

other similar goods as agreed by the parties. These goods will be supplied on FOB Chicago Airport (or other relevant destination) terms. All goods will be air freighted to customers within the territory concerned unless otherwise agreed. Any orders negotiated by the Agent shall conform to these terms.

(3)   The Agent will promote the sale of the Client's goods within the above-named territory exclusively. No sales are to be made outside of said territory or to third parties within his territory if they intend to export the goods outside of that territory.

(4)   The Agent shall not sell, or promote the sale of, competing goods within the named territory during the term of this agency agreement.

(5)   The Agent will disclose to all prospective buyers that he is acting as the Agent of the Client.

(6)   The Agent will forward all orders received by him to the Principal/Client for fulfillment. The Principal retains the right to reject any orders received if he so wishes.

(7)   The Agent will forward regular reports detailing his activities on behalf of the Principal. The content of such reports to be agreed by the parties.

(8)   The Agent shall not:

  (a) Pledge the credit of the Client without the authority of the Client.

  (b) Give any warranty or guarantee without the authority of the Client.

  (c) Sell any Product at a price that differs from those stated by the Client without the authority of the Client.

  (d) Accept any money on behalf of the Client without the authority of the Client

  (e) Incur any debt, or obligation, on behalf of the Client without die authority of the Client. (In each case any such authority must be in writing from the Client.)

(9)   The Agent shall receive a commission of 12% on all payments received by the Client for orders obtained by the Agent, or in the Agent's territory, for the duration of this

Agreement. The commission shall be based upon the FOB invoice price of the goods. Such commission will be paid to the

Agent within 30 days following receipt of payment for goods by the Client.

(10)   The Agent shall be reimbursed by the Client for any costs directly incurred by the Agent on behalf of the Client, for instance advertising costs, promotional printing or overseas travel. Written authority to incur such costs must be given in advance by the Client.

(11)   This agreement shall be governed by and constructed in accordance with the federal laws and laws of your state.

Signed on behalf of AT.C. Suppliers Inc. (Principal/Client)

Dated: 15 November 2002

Signed. Tom Maxwell (Agent)

Dated: 15 November 2002

6.11 Notes on this Agreement:

(a) Sole agency agreements are obviously preferable as they secure the agent in his territory. It is therefore important that the agreement states clearly that you are the sole agent of the client in that territory. If that is not mentioned then you should contact the principal/client and ask for it to be added to the agreement.

(b) It is sometimes the case, however, that agreements are specific to certain buyers or even certain transactions covering a period of time. In rare instances the agreement may cover just one specific contract, although this is usually reserved to large industrial contracts. Even in these instances a written agreement gives the agent that additional security.

(c) Another point to bear in mind is the situation where orders received from your area are for delivery outside of that territory. This is sometimes the case, for example where the goods are consigned to a branch office of the buyer. If this event is likely to arise then it is worthwhile having a clause inserted in the agreement at the beginning to protect your commission on such orders.

(d) An often expressed fear of agents is that they will lose the business once the supplier and buyer start to communicate directly with each other or become aware of each other's identity. This is not the case. Agents fulfill a very important function in the world of international trade and they are very much respected by both supplier and buyer alike. The saving of their commission is not worthwhile to the supplier as it will probably cost him more in time and effort than he will save in commission.

You can, however, ask that a clause be added to the agreement safeguarding your commission this would state that you will receive commission payment on all orders achieved in your territory even if they are passed directly to the client by the customer.

(e) The Principal/Client cannot break the agreement and appoint a new agent to the territory during the term of the agreement.

(f) The agent should normally receive his commission on all orders received from the territory by the client. This is regardless of whether the orders are forwarded throat the agent or not. The agent will need to monitor this to ensure that he is being notified of orders placed directly with the client. Most clients will automatically do this as they recognize that a good relationship with the agent is in their own best interest.

(g) TIP if you check back regularly with the potential buyers you have contacted then you can pick up more orders.

(h) Sometimes sales targets to be achieved by the agent are included in agreements. Try to avoid this as it will apply unnecessary pressure on you. It is more usual for targets to be agreed separately between client and agent, and this is to be preferred.

(i) The agreement may include a clause stating that copies of all types of correspondence such as letters/faxes/telexes and reports must be forwarded to the client. This does not present a problem as it would normally happen anyway.

(j) The expression 'pledge the credit of the Client' means that you cannot make financial commitments on behalf of your Principal. For example, you cannot order goods on behalf of your client without the client's consent.

(k) The Principal may well refuse to accept orders if they present a poor credit risk or there is insufficient profit margin on the sale or the goods are technically too different from the norm.

(l) If an order taken by you in any way conflicts with the terms of the agreement then you must seek the specific approval of the client before accepting the order.

The above example agreement would be quite acceptable to most clients and agents so you can use this as a suggested layout.

GOODS ON CONSIGNMENT

Some agents actually hold stocks of their client's goods so that orders received can be fulfilled locally rather than by shipment from overseas. This has obvious advantages for both buyer and seller. The buyer gets his goods faster and without the risk of 1055 or damage during shipment. The seller is released from the problem of frequent small shipments, making instead one substantial shipment at regular intervals to maintain adequate stocks at his agent's location.

You also receive benefits from this arrangement. You will receive either a higher rate of commission, or the right to sell at your own price making a profit on the sale. Also your volume of sales will probably increase because you can offer supply straight from stock. The agent, however, play a more important role in this situation, as we will see below.

a) Storage

You will need to acquire space for storing your client's goods when goods are supplied on consignment basis. If the Product is Jewelry or some ether Product that requires little storage space then probably you can arrange storage at your own home or office. If the Product is larger, for example furniture or electrical goods, then you may need to find a warehouse for storage purposes. Remember that even small items such as Jewelry may need to be kept secure from damage or theft. Warehouse space, if required, can be rented fairly cheaply through local commercial property agents.

b) Insurance

You will be held responsible for the goods entrusted to you on consignment. You will therefore need to arrange insurance for the goods both while being stored and while in transit to customers. This costs money and you must ensure that your commission or revenue on sales of the goods allows for these extra expenses.

c) Importation

This means clearing the goods through Customs and paying any required import duty and taxes. Alternatively, the goods can be placed into a 'bonded' warehouse until they are sold the duty and taxes being paid at that time. Customs procedures and importation-exportation can be arranged through a shipping agent.

d) Payment Terms

The relationship between Principal and agent also changes in the situation where goods are supplied on consignment. For example, the supplier may well invoice you for the goods granting a period of credit, say 90 days, in which you can sell the goods to your customers. This is not always the case, often you will not pay for the goods yourself, but rather the contract will still be created between buyer and seller with you taking your commission. In this case you are merely storing the goods on behalf of your client; if you are required to pay directly the supplier for the goods then you must be prepared to commit yourself to making that payment on time. Therefore, you should only consider accepting goods on consignment if you are sure of making a reasonably quick sale. This also relates to the Products concerned. Fast-moving consumer goods, for example books will obviously be a better risk than high-tech industrial machinery or specialized Products such as welding equipment, scientific instruments etc. where sales are more infrequent.

6.12 Setting up a Consignment Goods Facility

It is not difficult to set up a consignment goods facility and it can prove very rewarding especially if you can re-sell at your own price rather than that fixed by the supplier. If you are thinking of approaching your client with this suggestion then first consider all the points rose above to ensure that you have the facilities to manage the situation. In your letter you should point out the benefits to the supplier; this should be your first paragraph. These benefits include a larger volume of sales, fewer shipments, less administration and smaller inventories (stock) at his location. Follow this with a description of how you will physically handle the goods when they arrive, for instance Customs clearance, duty, taxes, storage, local distribution, insurance and so on to reassure the supplier as to your ability to manage this operation. Suggest that he sends you a 'trial' shipment of a small quantity - this gives you the advantage of a trial run as well!

One final word - when handling consignment goods:

- you should either receive a higher than normal rate of commission
- Or you should be allowed to re-sell at your own, price.

7.0 Buyer Research

7.1 Who Buys the Product?

First, who in the widest sense is the buyer or possibly it is a product that is purchased by everyone. To which group or groups does the product most appeal?

Secondly, who as individuals, or companies, buy the product and are the customers? There are a number of ways to tackle this research.

There is a great deal of research material available with regard to who buys a product, and much of this material is free. The following sources have already been mentioned in the chapters on setting up as an import or export agent so here we will not go into great detail about their services.

- US Department of Commerce - local institutions for promoting trade.

- Trade Association - industry-specific organizations for promoting trade.

- Public libraries

- Major international banks

- Newspapers and magazines

- Trade publications

- Internet

You can also contact market research companies who will carry out the task for you. However, this can be both expensive and, in our opinion, unnecessary at this stage of your business. Far better to do the job yourself and save the cost

What you are seeking in this mass of information is the names and addresses of potential buyers for the product or service you are promoting. It should be an easy task to create a lengthy list of names to contact - this will be your basic database for follow-up. Other information that may drop out of this research includes:

(a) The type of buyer: industrial or consumer.

(a) If it is an industrial market, the size of the buying company, the regularity of purchase, the quantity bought over a given period, say the past three years and soon. If it is a consumer market, then details such as age group, sex and income level can be relevant.

(b) The competing brands on the market

(c) The average price paid for the product

(d) The channel of sale: Retail, distributor, dealer or mail order.

(e) The method of promotion used to sell the product: for instance mail-shot, magazine advertising other general information on the product and its market place: for instance technical details

7.2 Why Do They Buy It?

The answer to this question isn't as obvious as it looks. What we mean by the question is do they buy it out of necessity, out of habit, or for industrial use, or do they buy it as a luxury? What we are trying to discover is the basic reason for the purchase, for instance the motivation. This is very important because once you know the answer to this you know how to 'position' the product in the market place. By 'position' we mean how you present the product to the market not so much in a physical sense as in a theoretical one. How do you want the customer to perceive the product? You want it to have the widest possible appeal, and that's where 'positioning' comes in.

Let us take a simple example. You invent a substance that removes any form of paint from fabrics. It would be commercially rather unwise to 'position' the product solely as aid for professional artists, hence excluding the rest of the population who at some time or other would use a product like that. You would position it as a 'magic' substance for everyday use in the home and possibly do an up-market pack for the artist community as a separate exercise. Let us give you some examples of products purchased under the above categories:

- Out of necessity:

  Basic foodstuffs, clothes, toiletries, household goods such as crockery, cutlery and cooking utensils.

- Out of habit:

  Alcoholic products, make-up, some medical products such as vitamin pills.

- For industrial use

  Raw materials and engineering products such as machine pads, tools, components.

- Luxury goods:

  Fashion goods, records, books, televisions, hi-fl stereo equipment, perfumes.

7.3 When Do They Buy It and How Often Do They Buy It?

Another essential piece of the puzzle is to know how often the product is purchased by a particular customer. Clothes will probably be purchased several times a year by the average person, for instance regular, repeat buying. On the other hand, a piece of machinery such as a power drill may only be purchased once every three to five years. You need to establish whether your product is going to enjoy:

(a) Regular, frequent sales to the same customer base or

(b) Occasional sales to different users with long intervals between sales to the same customer.

Also, are the sales seasonal? Fashion goods certainly are, as are some sports goods. When you think of all the things that people purchase at Christmas time you will realize just how seasonal some of those products are.

7.4 How Much Does Price Influence Demand for the Product?

We have already touched on this subject above. What happens to product sales when price increases? Do they fall noticeably or only slightly? This is called in economics The elasticity of demand' and is closely associated with the law of supply and demand which states that "as supply increases price falls and demand consequently increases until a balance is reached". The balance is when demand exactly matches supply with a fixed price. This balance is rarely achieved and usually the supply and demand for a product are in a constant state of change especially in a free economy.

By studying available market information you should be able to establish the position for your product and this will enable you to ensure that your pricing strategy is right for the market. This assumes that the supplier has allowed you some discretion with regard to pricing of the product. If the prices are fixed by him then you have to sell at that price.

There are a number of ways that you can tackle the construction of a pricing strategy.

- You can establish the price of competing products and pitch your price somewhere are within the range of the competitors. You may think that this will restrict your sales and that it would be better to pitch the price as low as you can afford to go while still achieving your usual commission and a profit fix your client. Not so, the average price achieved in the market place is the price most people expect to pay, otherwise it wouldn't be the average therefore you can enter the market with an equivalent product at that pricing level and still expect to achieve sales to your targeted level while achieving a better profit.

- You can project your product as a higher quality model and set the price higher than the competitors. In fact, setting a price higher than the norm suggests to the consumer that the product is of a higher quality. This is a very successful selling policy adopted by many companies. You keep the price high and suggest to the end-user that by paying less for a competing product they will end up with an inferior quality. This may or may not be true but the thought takes hold in the buyer's mind. There is also the 'snob' value effect with some consumer goods where people actually boast about paying more for a product, implying that they got the best!

- You can do the 'bargain basement' routine, you sell at a lower price than the competition, and you do away with the fancy wrapping and presentation. Another successful selling trick is appealing to the bargain hunters. A smaller profit margin per unit is achieved but your overall sales increase so the absolute (total) profit (and your commission) is higher.

7.5 What Do Customers Think of Competing Products?

By researching the levels of sales achieved by competing products you will be able to establish a league table of the most popular descending to the least popular. You can then take that research one step by finding out why one enjoys greater popularity. Is it quality, price, after-sales service, brand name, advertising, technical specification, packing or presentation? The easiest way to tackle this type of research is to compare the features of the competing products, either by reading the advertising literature or by obtaining the products and trying them out, this comparison will usually give you a good indication of why one product is top of the league.

Another way of tackling this issue is to send a carefully drafted questionnaire to a sample user-base this can be easily included with one of your promotional mailings to save in postage.

Sample questionnaire:

This should be sent to at least fifty users (or buyers) of the product if you are going to get any result at all. People are notoriously bad at filling in and returning questionnaires and a ten to twenty per cent return can be considered good.

The purpose of the questionnaire should be stated - for instance what you are trying to find out. It also helps if you offer some inducement to complete the form, for example a small gift.

Generally speaking names can be omitted from these questionnaires as it is the answers that are important, not who the people are.

The questionnaire should be designed to obtain the following information:

- The nature of the buyer's business - for instance wholesale, retail, distributor, dealer or industrial workshop.

- The region or county where the company is located. (If the questionnaire is being sent abroad, then the town or city would prove more useful.)

- The number of employees in the company. (This gives you an idea of the size of the company.)

- The quantity, or value, of the product concerned that the buyer purchases monthly or annually.

- List all the known suppliers (or the make) of the product and ask the reader to mark those suppliers or product brands that he currently uses or buys.

- Why they purchase that particular product.

- Would they consider changing supplier and, if so, why?

- Did price influence their purchasing decisions above everything else?

- Any other relevant information required.

End by thanking them for completing the questionnaire. Remember to keep the form short as long forms tend to put people off and they will often discard them. They won't spend more than ten minutes on it, so that is a good guide to how long it should be.

7.6 How Can the Market be Expanded?

Business planning

One of your areas of responsibility is to draw up a sample plan for the Principal/Client's sales in your territory. This means demonstrating to yourself (and to your client) how you expect to penetrate the market and how you will achieve unit sales of the product or service. However, this will not usually be necessary until you have been appointed as his agent.

Ideas

The second area is the ideas department! Part of any occupation is using your imagination. Spend one or two hours each week with a blank sheet of paper and a pencil and just jot down all the ideas that come to you, no matter how crazy they may seem at the time. Often you will get one or two genuine nuggets out of this, and it is part of your job as an agent to advise your client upon ways to expand the market and consequently your commission.

7.7 How to Create your Prospects List?

Extract information from your research to give you a list of potential buyers. These are called prospects' in sales terms. The more prospects you have, the more transactions you are likely to secure, so you can never have too many!

There are three parts to this exercise and it would be useful for you to actually start doing this now while you are studying this section. The three parts are:

(a) Extract names, addresses, phone numbers and other relevant information.
(b) Prepare individual cards for each prospect.
(c) File cards, either physically or electronically if you have a computer.

Now we will study each in turn:

a) Extract details

• Assemble all of your research material that you have acquired to date. This includes magazines, newspapers, directories, letters, faxes etc., in fact everything that has a potential buyer mentioned within it. Go through every item carefully and highlight the relevant details of prospective buyers. At the same time dispose of any material that is not useful for your agency - don't hoard useless information!

b) Prepare index card

• Purchase 500 white, ruled, index cards and a plastic, flip-top card holder. On each card write (preferably print) the name of the company or individual prospect, their address, phone and fax number, the product they are interested in and any other relevant information. Again, make sure that it is relevant information - these are working tools not detailed reports.

c) File cards

• File each card either in alphabetical order or 'p some other format that is meaningful for you. Color codes them if you wish.

• Alternatively, if you have a computer, file this information electronically in such a way that you can sort it by different criteria, for instance alphabetically by customer name, geographically by country or by product item.

You now have an essential toolbox of prospective buyers - this is your business in one small box, look after it and use it! If you have completed this exercise, well done!

7.8 Finding Buyers

7.8.1 Where to Start?

Over a period of months you, as agent, may need to write a good number of letters to promote your product and convert your prospects to real buyers. Not all of these will lead to business, but the ones that do should prove successful enough to earn you a very good living. So the first lesson is, the more sales approaches (by letter or fax) you make, the more you will achieve and the more you will earn.

Go to your card index and extract 10 cards, these are your work in progress for today. Now follow the steps outlined below.

1. The Daily Task

(a) Your first and foremost responsibility each day, whether you are doing this full time or part time, is to contact your prospects (your potential buyers). This should, wherever possible, be done first before you do anything else in your business each day. You must discipline yourself to do this every working day.

(b) Therefore take the ten cards that you have selected from your card index or contacts file and place them on your desk or table. Today you are going to either write to or fax each of these people.

2. Sales Statistics

Get yourself a diary or notebook and record for each day the following information:

- Number of letters written; faxes and telexes sent
- Number of contacts made; replies received
- Number of inquiries received
- Number of orders received
- Number of sales made
- Amount of commission earned
- New prospects found - transfer details to prospects cards

At first obviously you will only be completing the first item. As time goes by you will eventually have information to complete in each of the sections. These statistics are very important to your business.

3. Statistical Analysis

As your daily statistics build up you will be able to analyze them to give you valuable information about your business. You will be able to know that if you increase your number of approaches, the number of sales will increase proportionately. You will be able to tell how much average commission you make per transaction, how long it takes for an approach to turn into an order and so on.

4. The Golden Rule

The Golden Rule is 'Never stop contacting your potential buyers'. To achieve this all you need to do is discipline yourself to do two things each working day

- Find two new prospects
- Make two new approaches

Eventually you may need to change this number to four or six depending upon the statistical analysts of your own success. Time and experience will provide that information. Start today!

7.8.2 Promoting your Product

Sustained promotion keeps your product, and your name in front of the potential buyer. You can achieve a reasonable amount of promotion for very little cost if you set about it in the right way. Where promotion is concerned, there is little difference between the promotion of an imported product and that of a domestically produced product. The methods and costs are basically the same. There may need to be sonic modification of existing sales literature if it has been designed abroad. For example, language translation or technical specification amendments.

Overseas promotion of a product can be significantly different from domestic promotion. The main area of difference is the 'sales channel'. The channels used for promoting a product in your country may not necessarily be the best method for an international market.

7.8.2.1 Direct Mailing

Direct mailing means quite simply sending letters, literature or brochures through the post to potential buyers. Let us look at the approach through direct mailing; for example 50 potential buyers which you have compiled while carrying out your market research.

If you want to send a mail-shot to these 50 prospects then there are a number of items to be arranged. The ideal mail-shot will contain three pieces of literature and will arrive on the desk of the recipient early in the week - try not to have mailings arriving on a Friday.

(a)   The covering letter

Below we give a an example of such a covering letter

We would recommend that these letters are individually typed as it looks better to the buyer. However, if you have access to a word-processor or a photocopier then you can use a standard format letter with just the name and address of the recipient changed for each one by typing in the details. It is preferable to use letter-headed paper as well, it looks more professional.

(b)   The brochure or technical leaflet

The simplest method of obtaining these is to ask your client for them. If you are doing a mail-shot and you have 75 potential leads then he is unlikely to object to giving you the leaflets! You can enclose the leaflets of more than one supplier if you wish, but not if they are for competing products as this will only confuse the buyer. If, however, your client has no leaflet then you will need to produce your own. This can be designed by you and then passed to a printer for reproduction. Alternatively, if you have access to a computer and desktop publishing facilities, you can print the brochure yourself the following guidelines will help you in this task.

For this literature black and white photograph reproductions are usually acceptable. If you have color ones available then so much the better. You will have to decide whether it

Sample direct-mail cover letter

MAXWELL IMPORT & EXPORT AGENCY

8992 West 59th Street

Suite 001

Chicago IL 60643 U.S.A.

Phone (312) 568-8421

Fax (312} 568-8421

28 October, 2002.

Tony Buyer Ltd.,

I, Main Street,

Newton,

South Australia

Dear Mr. Smith

Subject: Export of Industrial Tools

I see in this month's copy of Australian Banking News that you are seeking suppliers of quality precision industrial tools. We represent the interests of a manufacturer in the United States of such tools. We have attached copies of their relevant technical literature and a schedule of FOB Chicago prices for your assistance.

We look forward to your reply on this excellent range of products, or if you require further information then please let us know immediately.

We look forward to your reply and remain,

Yours sincerely,
(Signed)
Tom Maxwell
Maxwell Import & Export Agency

Creating color brochures shows the product to the best advantage. For example, it would be fairly useless to show fashion goods in monochrome (black and white), color would be essential.

The brochure should contain the following minimum information

- Product description.
- Photograph or illustration of the product - preferably during use dimensions and weight.
- Any technical information such as power supply
- Description of what the product does
- Main features of the product.
- Benefits of the product for the user.
- The name, address and phone or fax number to contact for further information.

The brochure should be printed on good quality paper and should, if possible, be produced by a printer rather than photocopied or typed.

The price list

You can of course use the suppliers price lists if they are suitable. Alternatively, you can construct your own and then have it photocopied or printed for you. A sample price list might look like this:

PRICE LIST (Sample)

October 2002

Product	Minimum qty.	Price
Leather jackets	100	$37.00 each

Leather trousers	200	$ 26.00 each
Loather handbags	100	$ 17.00 each
Leather gloves	300	$ 7.00 each
Leather wallets	400	$ 3.00 each
Key holders	600	$ 1.25 each

All prices FOB Chicago.

For further information on these products please contact Tom Maxwell Agency at 312-568-8421.

The mailing

Now that you have assembled the components of the mail-shot, you can set about the actual mailing.

- Obtain 50 strong, letter size envelopes. Please try to avoid folding the literature before pulling it into the envelope. Sales literature should lay fiat in the envelope, in logical sequence (for instance covering letter on top, leaflet next, price list last).

- Mail the completed envelopes, which should be addressed clearly either by the use of an adhesive label or by direct typing on to the envelope.

7.8.3   Newspaper Promotion

This can also prove a successful way of promoting your agency. If you are an import agent then there are two levels of promotion to explore.

(a) You can place a small classified advertisement in Regional Sunday papers in major cities. This will be more expensive than National newspaper advertising but it will reach a much larger audience.

The advertisements should appear in the classified business-to-business sections. Costs for this form of promotion are available upon request to the newspapers concerned. The response to this promotion may be from businesses that are seeking agents for their products, or from companies seeking supplies of the products concerned.

(b) You can advertise in the local newspapers for your area. These obviously have a more restricted circulation, but on the other hand promotion costs are much smaller. An advertisement in the classified sections (business services section) of these publications will still reach some potential buyers for your product. Promotion costs are again available upon request to the newspapers concerned.

Sample newspaper trade magazine promotion

We are import agents for a wide range of quality toys and games. We can supply any wholesale or retail requirement at very competitive prices. For detailed catalogues and price lists contact: Tom Maxwell Phone: 312-568-8421

7.8.4   Trade Magazine Promotion

One of the more successful methods of promotion is through magazines. There are many hundreds of magazines published weekly and monthly in most countries) which cover every conceivable type of interest. The ones that will prove of most value to agents are the specialist trade magazines. To find the names of these you can contact your local library which should have a list of journals and other trade publications. Once you have the name, address and phone number of the publisher you can contact them for advertising rates and procedures. These are usually stated in the magazine anyway. Ask for a free copy of a back Issue.

For overseas publications, contact the commercial sections of the embassies and consulates, They will be able to provide names, addresses, phone or flux numbers and possibly sample back issues of selected magazines.

When choosing a magazine for promotion it is important that you look a little further than just cost. Other factors to consider include:

(a)   Circulation - how many readers do they claim to have? Is it distributed world-wide?

(b)   Price of the magazine - is it distributed free, as many trade magazines are, or is there a charge for the magazine? Free distribution will probably reach more people.

(c)   Is it directed towards businesses or individuals? Some magazines are for the enthusiast or hobbyist and some are published for commercial readers.

(d)   Are they well produced? Are the print and photographs of good quality? You want to get good value for your money so choose carefully. You can be fairly confident that an advertisement placed in the relevant magazine will reach the attention of the right market. There are usually reply cards at the end of these trade magazines for the reader to complete if something of interest has been advertised in that issue, hence there is a real incentive for people to reply to this kind of advertising.

(e)   Costs of advertising vary considerably depending upon the type and size of the advertisement placed and the circulation of the magazine concerned. For example if you wanted to place an advertisement consisting of a few lines in the classified sections this could cost you as little as $50.

7.8.5 Trade Fairs and Exhibitions

These can prove an excellent method of promoting your agency business, or the products you are selling. There are numerous trade shows organized throughout the year covering nearly every industry you can think of Some of these shows (or exhibitions) are geared towards business-to-business selling, others are more geared for consumer selling, for instance the end-user.

These are all basically trade shows regardless of the differing names. You will see them advertised as shows, exhibitions, fairs, missions or even conferences, but the concept is the same in each case: show your product and elicit customer orders.

The business leads, and eventual orders, obtained by attending these shows can make the expense more than worthwhile. It is worth talking to your local Department of commerce about the opportunities in your locality. The cost of having a small stand at these local shows is often quite reasonable. You will be in direct contact with a good cross-section of the local business community. Several hundred to several thousand potential buyers will attend a three-day local trade show. Even if your supplier doesn't exhibit at these shows it is well worth attending as you can make useful business contacts there. Local shows are quite extensively advertised in the local press and outside conference centers, so keep a watch for them.

Free Promotion

There are possibilities of gaining free promotion for your agency, and these methods can prove very successful.

One method, if you are an export agent, is to write to the commercial section of the embassy of the country to which you wish to export. You detail briefly the nature of your business and the product you are promoting, with an outline of the type of buyer you are seeking. This information will then be passed back to the home country for circulation amongst the business community, or to be kept on file it~ case of inquires from buyers in that country. This costs you no more than a first class stamp!

A second method is to give a brief outline (note that it should always be brief, see sample letter below) of your business to the county's department of commerce that covers the area to which you are interested in exporting. They will often write this up in their magazine which enjoys a wide circulation among the members in the home country.

Third, you can sometimes get free press write-ups about your company, or the products you are promoting, especially at the local paper level, by writing to them. They are always keen for news items and this applies equally to magazines as well as newspapers. You will need to give them a brief and concise summary of who you are, what you do and which product you are promoting. They will want to know the benefits of the product and possibly how it compares with competitor products. They may require some technical information as well. This information would normally be handled by the business correspondent, or if it is a technical journal, the science correspondent. The result of this form of media coverage is to Increase awareness of your product and thereby attract buyers.

Sample teller to overseas Department of commerce

(By overseas Department of commerce in this context we mean the one that is resident in the country in which you are interested).

MAXWELL IMPORT & EXPORT AGENCY

8992 West 89th Street

Suite 001

Chicago IL 60643 U.S.A.

Phone (3l 2) 568-8421

Fax (312) 568-8421

28 October, 2002.

(Insert name and address of overseas Department of commerce.)

Dear Sirs,

Subject: Trade with (insert country name)

May I take this opportunity of introducing myself'? I am an international trade agent specializing in woodcraft products. I would very much like to make contact with importers and exporters in (insert country name) who are involved in this trade so that we might promote trade between our two countries.

My company has been successful in establishing markets for woodcraft products in several European countries. Currently I represent three major manufacturers of woodcraft products.

I would be grateful if you would be kind enough to circulate this information through your magazine and national chambers of commerce so that contact can be established.

Regards,

(Signed)

Tom Maxwell

Maxwell Import & Export Agency

7.8.7   World Wide Web/Internet Marketing

No form of new media has gripped the imagination of consumers and marketers more than the Internet (the Net). It is the modem descendant of a government and academic computer network started two decades ago. The Net is a vast, global network of 345,000 interconnected computer networks, which are able to seamlessly connect an estimated 320 million users worldwide. No one owns the Net, and no organization or government controls it. The fiercely independent, yet cooperative nature of the Internet is one of its most prominent features.

The Net includes a series of different applications. E-mail is the most common of these applications. It allows people to instantly communicate across networks and vast reaches of the Internet. Usenet is a series of more than 60,000 discussion groups where users with similar interests share ideas. E-mail groups (known, as listservs) are similar to Usenet, but they use e-mail for communication, rather than special Usenet readers.

For a direct marketer, the existence of such lists might seem like a great opportunity. They ate not the same as mailing lists in the traditional sense. Commercial applications in e-mail listservs and Usenet have been resisted.

Growth of new Net users has been estimated at 60-85 percent annually. Low-cost access, minimal regulatory constraints, and the wealth of information available have all contributed to this growth. Another recent growth spurt has come as the consumer on-line services have given their subscribers Net access. This has forever changed the perception of the Net as a strictly academic and research tool into a highly commercial media. Internet home page, discussion groups and newsgroup are very effective marketing tools especially for imports.

Other highly effective methods are telemarketing, bulk e-mailing and fax on demand, Please contact a marketing consultant if you are not sure of what to do.

7.9 Types of Buyer

7.9.1 Distributor

A distributor buys goods on his own account, usually direct from a supplier. Because they often purchase directly from the supplier it can prove difficult for an agent to make contact with a distributor. However, it is always worth trying, especially as they usually purchase in large quantities. Also, many distributors purchase from domestic suppliers and are unaware of the opportunities for selling goods from abroad. An agent can open up a useful business relationship by bringing these goods to the attention of the distributor.

Distributors may have exclusive rights to the sale of those suppliers' goods in the particular market concerned.

The distributor will arrange for the storage and display of the goods and their sale to buyers who may be dealers, wholesalers or retailers. He breaks down the large order that he purchases from the supplier into smaller quantities for these further links in the chain of sale. His payment is the profit he makes on the sale of the goods.

They assume the financial risk involved in the contract. The distributor is usually expected to hold a reasonable stock of the products involved. The supplier normally gives extended credit to the distributor, for instance sixty days from date of invoice and a generous level of discount on the price of the goods, for instance 45 per cent. This reflects the level of service that the distributor is offering the supplier, for instance storage, selling on in smaller quantities hence saving the supplier administration and the credit risks of multiple buyers, advertising, promotion, demonstration and soon.

Distributors are usually listed as such in the phone books under the relevant product or service section. Trade magazines for the industry concerned will normally show the major distributors as well. International distributors can be traced through the relevant embassy, or sometimes their advertisements can be seen in the business sections of the quality international newspapers and magazines.

7.9.2   Dealer

The dealer buys and sells goods on his own account, but at the same time acts as an agent for one or more suppliers. So again there is a client-agent relationship although often it is confined to domestic trade. This means that there are real opportunities for the commission agent to secure business with a dealer for imported products, or overseas, for exported products.

The payment the dealer receives is in the form of the profit made on his sales. Dealers are often customers of distributors. The general definition of distributor and dealer is quite confusing as the larger dealers often act like distributors. The most obvious way of telling the difference is by scale of operation. Distributors are normally committed to large purchases from the supplier arid operate on a much larger scale than dealers.

The supplier usually extends a period of credit for orders placed on him by dealers, for instance thirty days from date of invoice. This enables the dealer to manage his cash flow better and his business in general -which in the long run ensures greater sales of the supplier's products. Similarly there is usually a generous discount given to the dealer on the price of the goods, for instance 33 per cent. This reflects the close relationship between the supplier and the dealer, but at the same time is less than the discount received by distributors, who carry out a greater level of activity on behalf of the supplier.

7.9.3 Importer

An importer can actually be any other form of business such as a distributor, dealer, wholesaler or retailer. In this instance, however, we are talking about someone or a company who imports products for onward distribution through these other selling channels (by splitting bulk imports into smaller quantities). They are therefore of interest to commission agents as they represent large-scale buyers of imported products. Successful contact in this area can lead to large-volume transactions with resulting high levels of commission. Import companies are listed in the phone book and in international trade and telex directories.

7.9.4 Wholesaler

By wholesaler we mean someone who is acting as a middleman between a supplier or importer and a retailer. The wholesaler buys in bulk from a manufacturer or large-scale importer/distributor and then splits the goods into smaller purchase units for onward sale to retailers. The wholesaler adds a mark-up to the price for performing this service and that is how he makes his profit.

There are good opportunities here again for the commission agent as wholesalers will often purchase direct from supplier's abroad if the price is competitive.

7.9.5 Retailer

Retail outlets are those that are selling direct to the end-user. The end-user may be the housewife or proverbial 'man in the street', or it may be another business unit that uses the product in its own business activity. The retailer generates his profit by adding a mark-up to the price of the product that he has purchased from the wholesaler.

The best way to approach this channel is first to try the local retailers in your area, Find the ones who are selling the product you are promoting, using the phone book or going down to shopping areas See if you can interest them in taking your product.

Where export markets are concerned, you will need to go through the embassy or department of commerce of the country concerned who may have mailing lists available to them of large retailers for your industry.

7.9.6 Department Stores

The difference between the above selling channels is not always clear, as for example in the case of department stores. They are retail units and yet they also often fulfill the roles of wholesaler and importer as well. Many large department-store chains purchase centrally direct from the overseas manufacturer, and carry out the importing and wholesale activity within their own organization. This is not to say that there are not still opportunities here for the commission agent. Many of these large stores will still purchase through agents if the price is competitive and the product innovative. Contact should first be made to the Head Office Buyer of these stores. They will almost immediately be able to indicate to you whether your product and price will be of interest to them. Once again they will be looking for large quantities, supplied quickly and at the lowest possible prices.

7.9.7   End User

This is the end of the selling chain. The person who finally 'consumes' the product or service. This may be, as stated above, an individual or a company. The end-user is the source of the 'demand' for a product, if that demand does not exist then there will be no point in the production and selling process. The agent can sell to end-users direct. Many of the large 'corporate' companies are end-users of products and will purchase through agents. The type of product might be business machinery, manufacturing equipment or tools, personal computers, scientific instruments and so on.

The one-man purchaser who will buy a small quantity of a product through the agent should not be disregarded either. These small orders can be consolidated into one larger bulk shipment.

7.9.8   Mail Order

Commission agents can also sell directly through 'mail order' to the general public, combining the multiple one-off orders into one large order for forwarding to the client. Often you can actually purchase goods in a small quantity on your own account for re-sale to retailers, end-users and mail order buyers. This enables you to charge a price which generates profit for you as well as still achieving your commission from the client.

Another profitable method is to sell your product to mail order catalogue companies.

Mail order works as follows

The seller produces a catalogue, and/or places advertisements, offering his goods for sale. There are usually pictures of all the products being offered so that the prospective buyer can see what he is getting. This is very important as in mail order the buyer cannot actually see the goods before he sends for them. The price of the goods is also shown as well as postage and packing or delivery charge. The buyer then fills out the order form, encloses his check/postal order for the goods, and sends them away by post. The goods are then sent to him within twenty-one days by the mail order company. If the buyer is not happy with the goods then in most cases he has the right to return the goods and receive a full refund providing he does so within twenty-eight days of receipt of the goods. It is a very effective method of selling that has grown to mammoth proportions in the United States market.

Sample contact letter to a mail order company

MAXWELL IMPORT & EXPORT AGENCY

8992 West 89th Street

Suite 001

Chicago IL 60643 U.S.A.

Phone (312) 568-8421

Fax (312) 568-8421

28 October, 2002.

ABC Mail Order Catalogue

ABC House

Massachusetts, USA

For the attention of the purchasing Manager

Dear Sir:

Subject: Superior quality linens

I represent a company based in France which manufactures a range of beautiful linen products. These are made by traditional methods and are of the finest quality. I have enclosed a descriptive brochure for your reference.

If you would wish to consider the marketing of this product through your catalogue in the United States then I am sure that we could arrive at a mutually beneficial agreement upon both price and quantity.

I look forward to hearing from you regarding your interest or to discuss the matter further.

Yours Faithfully,

(Signed)

Tom Maxwell

Maxwell (Imports & Export) Agency

When approaching mail order companies with a view to selling to them you will need to be well prepared. If you are to be successful you will need to have a good-quality product, competitive price and sufficient quantities of the product to satisfy mail order demand, witch can run into tens or even hundreds of thousands of units.

You can adapt the above letter to address a mail order company in some other country or for a different product. You can find out details of mail order companies overseas by contacting the relevant embassy (commercial section) of the country concerned or through the country's Department of commerce.

8.0 Building up Your Agency

8.1 How the Relationship Starts

Your first contact with the buyer was in the form of correspondence, a letter sent by you with the relevant price lists and brochures. His reply may have requested further information concerning the products, for example, technical details, price discounts, quality details and soon. At this stage he is probably still undecided about whether or not to purchase the product.

The next step is to follow up with a further letter, a phone call, telex or fax. In any form of business you need persistence; it is a continual process of bringing the products you are dealing in to the attention of the prospective buyer. This needs to be done in a planned and structured way

8.2 A Marketing Plan

The creation of an effective marketing plan (for instance what you intend to sell, how you intend to sell it, and to whom you intend to sell it) as part of your total business plan is of importance for a number of reasons.

1. It gives you a plan to work to and goals to achieve. Your business will be going in a certain direction rather than being tossed about on the waves of chance.
2. It inspires confidence in your client. If you can demonstrate to him that you have a clear plan and direction, he will be more prepared to support your efforts.
3. It demonstrates a planned sales and marketing policy to your prospective buyers. This inspires confidence in the products you are promoting - you are putting a great deal of effort into selling them and this proves your confidence in the product.

8.3 Creating a Marketing Plan

You want to accomplish a number of goals.

(a) What product(s) are you going to promote? Which Product?

(b) What methods are you going to use to promote the product? What do you need to do this effectively in the way of materials and outside services such as mail-shots and printers?

(c) What is the market for the product and approximately of what size is that market? Identify the individual persons or companies that are the target customers.

This needs to be translated into specific intentions, action plans and anticipated revenue. Let us see how this can be done.

Sample Marketing Plan

For your assistance let us look at a simple example of a marketing plan for the export of kitchenware. Let us assume that you have been given an export agency for kitchenware going to the Canada. You can think of a marketing plan as the four P's Product, Promotion, Place and Price. The first six-month marketing plan may look something like this

1.   Products

The product range will consist of high-quality made in U.S. products, namely stoneware crockery, stainless steel cutlery, electrical kitchen equipment and certain specialized articles such as wall clocks, bone-china dinner services and 'antique' giftware. The emphasis will be on quality.

2.   Methods of promotion.

A direct mail-shot to major retail and wholesale outlets will take place during the next six weeks to raise awareness of the products. Wherever possible we will use the supplier's basic material.

3.   Territory and contacts.

Initially the target area will be Quebec and Ontario in Canada.

4.   Revenue targets:

The revenue target for the first six months of operation by product range is:

(a) Stoneware crockery: $20,000 per month (minimum order value = $10,000).

(b) Stainless steel cutlery: $15,000 per month (minimum order value = $7,500).

(c) Electrical kitchen equipment $25000 per month (minimum order value = $12, 500).

(d) Specialized products: 520,000 per month (no minimum order values to be applied).

Total revenue target for first six months of operation = $480,000

Commission rate -- 11%. Net commission therefore (for 6 months) = $52,800

Having drawn up this type of marketing plan you are now clear as to your approach to the market and the targets you wish to achieve for your agency. Next you need to translate the plan into action.

8.3.1 The Action Plan

Let us go a step further than the marketing plan and start to bring it to life in the form of activity that you need to take. You want to earn $52,800 commission over the next six months from this particular product range. To achieve this you need to sell $480,000 worth of product. How many sales is that?

Look at the plan:

Item A = 6 months revenue of $120,000. Assuming each order is at average value of $1,500 you will need to make 120,000/1500 = 80 sales.

Item B = 6 months revenue of $90,000. Assuming each order is at average value of $1,000 you will need to make 9, 0000/1000 = 90 sales.

Item C =6 months revenue of $150,000. Assuming each order is at average value of $1,500 you will need to make 150,000/1,500 = 100 sales.

Item D = 6 months revenue of$ 120,000. Assuming each order is at average value of $2,000 you will need to make 120,000/2,000 = 60 sales.

Therefore, in total, you will need to make a maximum of 330 sales transactions to achieve your commission goal of $52,800. (It would take fewer sales to reach your target if the average order value for each item was higher than those given in the example.) The next step is to calculate how much letters (or faxes) you will need to send/write to potential buyers to achieve your targeted sales over a six-month period. When you have built up some sales statistics you will have real information to use, but for now you will have to make some assumptions. Let us assume that it takes ten approaches to achieve one sale. Therefore you will need to make up to 3300 approaches to achieve the required level of sales. Now you know the task you can set about achieving your goal.

8.2 What the Buyer will Expect

The buyer will expect a number of things from you even though you are not working for him and the primary relationship is between your client and the buyer.

(a) He will expect literature and price lists. Buyers want to see what they are going to buy, including specifications, features, technical data, prices and terms. They want it well presented in an easily understood format. It is pad of your responsibility to ensure that you have this material available, whether it is supplied by your client or produced by yourself

(b) He will expect an efficient service in response to his queries or requests for further information. It is important that you answer his letters, faxes or phone calls urgently. You should always try to reply to letters within two or three days of receiving them and phone calls should always be answered within 24 hours. If you are going away on vacation or on business, try to get someone you can trust to take phone messages for you and open the mall while you are gone. If you can phone them a couple of times while you are away, this will give you the chance to deal with anything urgent that has cropped up. You will at least be able to phone any customers who need your attention. The buyer won't accept your being on vacation as an adequate excuse.

(c) He will expect you to act as an intermediary between him and your client. Much of the contact may be made directly between the two parties, but there may still be a requirement for your involvement, especially in the early stages, for example in negotiating on the terms of the contract.

8.3 What you can Expect from the Buyer

Basically, you can expect regular information on the progress of the order and notification of any problems that may arise. As you will often be the person on the spot it is natural for the buyer to talk to you and to ask your advice on matters relating to the order. If you can establish a strong enough relationship with the buyer then it may be possible to get from him a wealth of useful information concerning his purchases

- Does he purchase from competitive sources?
- Does he import all his requirements or are some supplied domestically?
- What are his total annual purchases of the product?
- Is his trade seasonal?
- This will assist in your planning of future sales to the same buyer.

8.4 Growing the Relationship

Usually your buyer will be sufficiently pleased with his initial order for the product that he will place repeat orders through you. This enables you to build an on-going relationship with the buyer, which will become as important as the relationship you have with your client. Generally once you have established yourself with a buyer and he feels confident of future business, the process of selling becomes easier. People like to deal with someone they know and can rely upon; you need to build this type of relationship

Provided that you have fulfilled the first delivery and the buyer is happy with the product then further orders are very likely. This does not mean that you can stop bothering with the account and just wait for the orders to roll in. You will always have to work at ensuring the buyer is satisfied and knows you are there to help if required.

There are a number of practical ways in which you can assist the creation of this agent-buyer relationship. Occasionally invite the buyer out to lunch if he is based locally. This may be the owner of the company if it is a small business or the purchasing manager if it is a larger concern. You don't need to do this frequently; a couple of times or even once a year should be adequate. Obviously, you will not be able to do this if you are acting as an export agent, as the buyer will be based abroad. However, you can still contact him by letter at regular intervals and make sure that you establish a personal relationship.

Always respond to correspondence quickly and efficiently. Ensure that your information is correct, and keep the buyer informed of the progress of his order. In most cases your client will notify him of shipping dates and shipment details but check to make sure this has happened and if not find out the necessary information for him.

Keep your buyers informed of new products, or improved versions of existing products, that have become available. Send them brochures and price lists on a regular basis

8.5 Introducing Companies to Overseas Trade

There are very many companies in America and throughout the world who have no involvement m international trade. They have a satisfactory domestic market and show little interest in getting involved in export/import business. These are prime candidates for the commission agent as you can show them the advantages of entering overseas trade.

These companies who are not exporting, or importing, can be researched in the same way as outlined earlier. One other method is to work through your local phone book looking at all the categories that include manufacturers, wholesalers and large retail stores. These are potential domestic exporters/importer. Many of them will probably already be active in overseas trade, but some won't to discover if they are or not you can either send them an introductory letter with a descriptive leaflet of your product or fax or phone them. When you have detected the non-active companies you can follow up with further correspondence or set up meetings with them to try to persuade them to enter overseas trade using your services.

8.6 Acquiring Additional Commissions

Another useful way of raising revenue which it is word, mentioning is asking shipping agents for a commission on any freight movement (and freight insurance contracts) you get for them. When you are arranging an export or import transaction for your client and buyer you simply suggest that they use a particular shipping agent for the carriage of the goods. Usually the shipping agent will pay a commission for any business that you obtain for them in this way.

8.7 The Sales Transaction

Although you, as an agent, will not actually be a party to the sale transaction between your client and the buyer, you nevertheless need a basic understanding of contractual terms and responsibilities, especially as they apply to international trade. You will be expected to negotiate the sale and obtain the order for your client; therefore you need to understand what you are doing and what the consequences are.

8.7.1   Information Inquiry

The initial contact that is received from a prospective buyer is termed the Inquiry this is a request for a specification of goods with corresponding prices. It may be received in response to advertising, or a mail-shot, or a specific letter you have written to a buyer or it may be the result of a personal visit made to the buyer. When you receive such an Inquiry it is essential that you act on it immediately. If you are in a position to answer the Inquiry yourself then do so immediately, within 48 hours. If you need to contact your client for further information then respond to the buyer immediately explaining that full details will follow shortly.

8.7.2 Quotation

The response you, or your client, make to the Inquiry is termed the quotation. The quotation is a detailed offer giving details of the products or services which are for sale. A sample quotation is given below for your guidance. This document can be prepared and sent either by your client or by yourself, but in either case it should be absolutely clear to the buyer that they are contracting with your client and not with you. It must be obvious to the buyer that you are acting solely as an agent. Usually a clause is added to the end of the quotation to this effect; for example:

Tom Maxwell acting as agent for ABC Trading (Far East) Ltd.
This is only applicable if you are preparing the quotation for your client

Supporting literature such as brochures, specifications and manuals may be attached to the quotation. At this stage you do not need to include a sample of the product unless specifically requested to do so in the buyer's inquiry Even then you will need to consider carefully your policy concerning providing samples. It is usually better to wait until you know that the customer definitely intends to buy. Obviously with many products you cannot provide samples anyway because of the cost, size or nature of the product. It really only applies to low cost, small, mass-produced items.

Sample quotation

(Showing a quotation from an oversea supplier to a US buyer,)

ABC Trading Far East) Ltd. Kowloon, Hong Kong

XYZ Chicago Inc.,

2202, 20th Avenue,

Chicago, IL, United States

1 July 2002

Quotation Number: ABC 1/7/02

Copy to: Tom Maxwell (Agency)

Dear Sirs,

With reference to your Inquiry of 24 June 2002 we have pleasure in presenting our quotation as follows:

QTY.	DESCRIPTION	UNIT PRICE US$	TOTAL PRICE US$
40 doz.	Porcelain vases, blue	2.10	1008.00
20 doz.	Porcelain dogs	1.25	300.00
45 doz.	Porcelain soup spoons	1,35	729.00
25 doz.	Porcelain birds	3.50	1,050.00
50 doz.	Porcelain rice bowls	2.00	1,200.00

Total: $4,287.00

Approx. l5 cartons, each 100 cm x 100 cm x 50cm.

Weight: each 16 kilos.

Terms: - All prices are FOB Hong Kong Airport.

- Air-freight charges payable at destination.

- Not insured by ABC Trading (Far East) Ltd.
- Payment by Irrevocable Letter of Credit.
- Quotation is valid for sixty (60) days from date of issue.
- Minimum purchase $1500.00 US Dollars.

This quotation is subject to our standard terms and conditions of contract. Signed on behalf of ABC Trading (Far East) Ltd

(a) When dealing with the Far East you will probably see most quotations in Dollars. Most Western European countries will trade in their own currency, for instance French Francs, German Deutschmark, and so on. Eastern European countries also tend to trade in their own currencies.

(b) The quotation should clearly demonstrate that the client is issuing the document and that he is the supplier under any eventual contract.

(c) Quotations should always be dated and should state the period until expiry.

(d) If the client is preparing the quotation a copy of it should be forwarded to you as the agent. If you are preparing the quotation then your client should be copied.

(e) The quotation should itemize quantities, description of goods, unit and total prices.

(f) Delivery terms must be stated, in this case FOB (Free on Board) Hong Kong Airport.

(g) It should be also clearly indicated who will be paying freight and insurance charges. In this case the buyer will pay and he will have to find out what additional cost this will add to the price of the goods.

(h) Payment terms should be clearly shown.

(i) The minimum value of purchase is often shown. This means that the supplier would not find it worthwhile to ship quantities below that value. This minimum purchase can be in value terms or quantity of units. Often the minimum is quite low, as in the example above, but in some cases it can be quite high, for instance $50,000. In that case it is always worth asking the supplier if he will accept a smaller order in the expectation of larger orders later. At the end of the day most suppliers are open to negotiation as any sale is usually better than none, providing it is commercially viable. Alternatively, you can put together several smaller orders to achieve the supplier's minimum transaction requirement.

(j) Payment could then be made for these directly by the individual buyers.

(k) The prices quoted should be what are actually required for the goods. Any reduction in these prices should only apply if large quantities are ordered by the customer. The quotation should always be signed by the sender.

8.7.3 Calculating Export Prices

We need to mention briefly at this stage the factors to consider when calculating export prices for goods Although this will normally be a job for your client, it is possible that you will have some discretion in preparing any quotations that you construct on behalf of your client.

(a) Materials

The total cost of materials use per unit product

(b) Utilities.

Energy supplied for the manufacturing process per unit product

(c) Labor

Manpower cost per unit product.

Equipment cost per unit

(d) Overheads

(e) Advertising

Any promotional or advertising expenditure will have to be recovered.

(f) Packing

The furniture, to use our above example, will need careful packing for export.

(g) Documentation

The preparation of export documentation, such as certificates of origin, will cost money which needs to be recovered. Delivery to the port

(h) Transport and insurance charges for taking the furniture to the docks or airport. Customs clearance

(i) Shipping agents will charge for any services performed in this area. These charges need to be recovered.

(j) Freight
Sea-freight, air-freight, road, rail or postal charges need to be added to the price if the exporter is paying these.

(k) Insurance
If the exporter is going to arrange the freight insurance contract, then he will need to recover the premium costs.
- On delivery charges
- If the supplier is paying for the goods to be on-delivered from the port or airport of arrival overseas to the buyer's location then again these costs need to be recovered.

(l) Commissions
   a) Any agency commission payable to you needs to be added to the selling price. Commission is paid on the FOB price of the goods

(m) Profit
- The profit will be the difference between costs and price.

Shipping, delivery and handling costs can be calculated for you by a shipping agent. He will also handle any documentation required

Example of export pricing

To assist you in calculating export prices let us look at an example incorporating the factors listed above.

Product: 100 video recorders going for export to India. CIF Madras

Cost per unit:

Raw materials and components:	$ 750.00
Fuel for heating and electricity:	$ 15.00
Labor for assembly:	$ 350.00
Capital equipment (spread over three years):	$ 75.00

(This is calculated by total capital costs per year divided by number of production units per year.)

Overheads:	$ 150.00

(This is calculated by total annual overheads divided by number of production units per year.)

Advertising costs (estimated):	$ 30.00
Packing:	$ 50.00
Documentation:	$ 5.00
FOB charges:	$15.00
Profit:	$1000.00
Sub total	$2440.00

Agent's commissions (at 8 per cent for example):	
8 per cent of $2440	$195.20
Customs clearance:	$12.50

Freight (Air-freight):	$30.00
Insurance:	$10.00
Total:	$2687.70
* Total sale price CIF Madras per unit:	$2687.70
* Total order value $268.77 x 100 units =	$268,770.00

Note: You may not be involved in this pricing process as usually this is done by the supplier, but you may be asked to contribute to the process of pricing, especially if the supplier is a newcomer to international trade.

8.7.4   The Order

The order document will confirm the information contained in the quotation and should agree in all respects. If it differs from the quotation in any way, which is sometimes the case, then your client will have to decide whether or not to accept the order as it stands, or issue an amended quotation. The difference could be in quantity, types, price, shipment methods, payment methods or delivery terms

The order usually takes the form of an official-looking document but this is not always the case, nor need it be to establish the contract. A letter stating that the customer accepts the quotation and looks forward to receiving the goods in fad constitutes an order, in fact anything which indicates acceptance of the quotation, including a telex, fax or phone call, constitutes an order from the customer and can be treated as such. Obviously a formal, written document is the safest way for all concerned as it is then very clear what terms and conditions apply to the contract.

The order may be sent to you or to the client direct. The normal procedure is fir the order to go to the agent who sent the quotation. It, however, the client sent the quotation the order will usually be sent directly to him. If the order is placed directly with your client then he will inform you of this. Often the agent's work ends at this stage and you sit back and await your commission which will be paid to you as soon as the client is paid by the buyer.

8.8 The Acknowledgement of Order

The final part of the formation of the contract is the acknowledgement of order to the customer. This again is usually a document, not unlike the quotation, which states clearly the terms and conditions of the contract as they relate to each party. This should be sent to the customer as soon as possible after receipt of his order so that there is no misunderstanding regarding the terms of the contract. Note that if at this stage the acknowledgement differs in some material fact from the customer order then you are in fact making a new offer to him and not accepting his order.

Delivery terms

Delivery terms are those that indicate who is responsible for delivery in a contract, at what point delivery takes place and at what point property (ownership) of the goods passes from one party, the supplier, to the other, the buyer. They also indicate who is responsible for arranging the contract of freight insurance. (Freight in this context covers any form of transport not just sea-freight.)

(a)   Ex-works (EXW)

This term means that the seller is only responsible for producing the goods (and possibly packing them for shipment). The buyer is responsible for collecting the goods from the supplier's location and for shipping them to his location overseas. He will either use the services of a shipping agent to carry out this function for him, or he will arrange it directly wit] the shipping line who will send in their carrier. The responsibility for the goods passes to the buyer at point of collection.

This term is not common nowadays as it is usually more difficult for the buyer to arrange these services than the supplier, who is based in the country of export.

(b)   Free carrier (FCA)

This term is a derivative of FOB and is applicable to goods shipped by road transport and rail shipment. In most other aspects it serves the same function as FOB.

(c)   Free alongside ship (FAS)

Another derivative of FOB, the difference being that the seller is only responsible for the goods up to the point of delivery alongside the carrying vessel.

(d)   Free on board (FOB)

This term is usually followed by the name of the seaport, or airport, of loading of the goods, for instance FOB Hong Kong Airport to use our earlier example. It means that the supplier is responsible for all activity invoking the goods, and for all costs incurred, up to the point of loading on to the ship or aircraft including insurance for the goods up to point of loading. After that point the buyer is responsible for the goods and for all costs incurred including freight and insurance.

This term is still in common usage in overseas trade although it is losing ground to CFR and CIF (see below). Both of these latter terms make it easier for the buyer as he knows the exact costs he will incur for the goods and he does not have to arrange the freighting of the goods.

(e)   Cost and freight (CFR)

This term is usually followed by the name of the port, or airport, of arrival in the country of destination, for instance CFR Chicago (0' Hare) Airport. It means that the supplier is responsible for the goods and for the freight charges up to the point of arrival at the named port or airport where responsibility passes to the buyer. However, he is not responsible for freight insurance, which is still the responsibility of the buyer. The buyer is also responsible for the goods, and charges, from the point of off-loading. Cost in this context means cost of goods supplied to FOB point plus the freight charge and is the amount the buyer will be invoiced.

(/)   Cost insurance and freight (CIF)

This term is again usually followed by the name of the port, or airport, of destination, for instance CIF Sydney. It differs from CFR in that the supplier, rather than the buyer, is responsible for arranging the contract of freight insurance for the goods. Insurance premiums are normally paid at the point at which the insurance policy is issued.

(g)   Carriage paid to (CPT.)

This differs from CIF terms in that the carriage is only paid to an agreed destination point, not necessarily to final destination. Also freight insurance is still the responsibility of the buyer.

(h) Carriage and insurance paid to (('IF,)

This differs from CPT in that the freight insurance becomes the responsibility of the seller.

(i) Delivered at frontier (DAF)

All responsibility for the goods rests with the seller up to the frontier of the importing country.

(j) Delivered ex ship (DES)

All responsibility for the goods rests with the seller up to the point of off-loading from the carrying vessel.

(k) Delivered ex quay (duty paid) (DEQ)

All responsibility for the goods rests with the seller up to the point of collection from the quay, including the import duty (if any)

(l)   Delivered duty paid (DDP)

This term is rarely used. It means that the supplier is responsible for delivery of the goods, and all related charges, up to the buyer's location in the country of destination. It is especially applicable to road transport methods where goods are collected from the supplier's warehouse and delivered to the door of the buyer, all charges en route being charged to the buyer. In some cases even import duty and VAT may be paid by the supplier at the Customs point, which is then charged back to the buyer by the supplier. There are a number of minor derivatives of this term:

(m) Delivered duty unpaid (DDU)

All responsibility for the goods rests with the seller up to the point of delivery to the buyer except for the payment of any import duty.

8.8.1 Which Delivery Term to Choose?

The best term to use for an international order depends upon whether you are the buyer or the seller. From the buyer's point of view delivered duty paid (DDP) or cost, insurance and freight (CIF) is best because these require the least amount of work on the part of the buyer. He need arrange nothing other than, in the case of CIF, delivery from the port of arrival. He can be certain of receiving fair shipping and insurance charges from the supplier because the amount charged by the carrier (airline, shipping line, road carrier or railway authority) is stated on the document of shipment and he can compare this with the invoice he has received. Similarly, insurance premiums will be stated on the policy.

From the supplier's point of view ex-works is the easiest term because all he has to do is advise the buyer that the goods are ready for collection. FOB and its derivatives are also attractive.

However, the supplier will usually comply with the wishes of the buyer in this regard because he wants him to be happy with the service provided.

9.1 Financial Considerations

9.1.1 Payment Terms

First let us look at the most commonly used methods of paying for overseas orders. It will suffice to give you a working knowledge of the subject so that you understand the implications of each method of payment.

The payment terms used for any particular order are the subject of negotiation between buyer and seller, or between buyer and agent. However, it is the seller who will have the final say on what the terms are for it is he who supplies the goods and requires payment.

Other factors which can influence the method of payment are:

1. The custom of the trade for the product, for example open account terms are common in the sale of consumer goods.

2. The countries of destination, for example irrevocable letters of credit are the norm for trade with some Asian countries.

3. The value of the goods. Generally speaking, the higher the value of the order the more secure the payment terms.

4. The period of credit to be extended to the buyer. If the supplier is offering extended credit terms, for instance 90 days, then often a bill of exchange will be used.

5. The method of shipment. If sea-freight shipment is being used then extended payment terms may be offered to allow for the time lapse until arrival of the goods at destination.

9.1 Cash with Order

This is sometimes referred to as 'cash in advance', meaning cash in advance of shipment. It is the safest method of payment as far as the supplier is concerned. He receives the payment with the customer order and can then proceed to ship the goods. It is usually used for small value orders or where the parties have not previously traded and are unaware of each other's financial standing. The cash is transferred in the form of a banker's draft, international check, postal order (for small amounts), and credit card or by bank transfer.

9.2 Letter of Credit

This is one of the safest methods of payment for an overseas order. It is often used where the parties to the order have not previously traded with each other or where the custom for that country dictates. A letter of credit is an instruction by the buyer to his bank to make funds available to the supplier through a bank in his county providing certain documents (called 'shipping documents') are presented by the supplier by a specified date. Hence there is security for both the supplier (his payment) and the buyer (shipment of the goods). This is the most secure method of payment, provided that the documents presented to the bank by the supplier are correct.

9.2.1   How a 'Letter of Credit' Works?

The supplier requests payment by irrevocable letter of credit (see below) from a buyer that you, the agent, have introduced. The buyer goes to his bank and completes the required application form, giving details of the order. The bank ensures that adequate fluids have been deposited in the buyer's account to cover the letter of credit amount, or that he has a sufficient overdraft facility to cover the amount.

The bank then draws up the official letter of credit document which will contain the following information:

(a) The name and address of the applicant, the buyer.

(b) The name and address of the beneficiary, the supplier.

(c) The name and address of the 'opening bank', for instance the bank that opens the letter of credit for the buyer.

(d) The value of the letter of credit, and the currency.

(e) The expiry date, by which time shipment must be made, with a further date (usually 10 to 15 days later), by which time the shipping documents must be presented by the supplier to the advising bank in his country

(f) How payment will be made to the supplier, for instance against presentation of shipping documents, or 30 days after presentation of shipping documents.

(g) The description of the goods, including quantity.

(h) The method of shipment to be used.

(i) The shipping documents to be presented, which must be originals unless otherwise stated.

Any special conditions that the buyer may require, for example if he requires a particular routing for the product when shipped.

This document is forwarded to the supplier via the bank in his country (called the 'correspondent' or advising' bank) The supplier checks the document to ensure first that it is correct and second that he can comply with its conditions. If there is anything that he disagrees with then he should communicate this immediately, both to the advising bank in his country and to the buyer, so that the letter of credit can be amended accordingly. The amended letter of credit should still be checked thoroughly before shipment takes place.

When shipment of the goods takes place the supplier prepares the shipping documents exactly in accordance with the letter of credit and presents them to the advising bank for payment upon the due date. If they are correct then the advising bank will pay the supplier if it is a confirmed letter of credit (see below) or will send them onto the opening bank in the buyer's country if the letter of credit is not confirmed. The 'opening' bank (see (c) above) will then transfer the funds to the 'advising' bank (see previous paragraph) for forwarding to the supplier. The documents are then released to the buyer so that he can gain possession of the goods.

9.2.2   Types of 'Letter of Credit'

Letters of credit come in a number of different forms. The form to be used will be negotiated between buyer and seller at time of entering the contract. The types are:

1. Revocable:

This is rarely used nowadays. This means that the buyer can revoke the letter of credit (for instance cancel it) at any time up to point of shipment of the goods.

2. Irrevocable:

The most common type of letter of credit. This is the type that can be recommended in most cases. The letter of credit is irrevocable, which means it cannot be cancelled or amended without the approval and specific written agreement of both parties to the order.

3. Confirmed:

This will either be a confirmed revocable or a confirmed irrevocable letter of credit. It means that the bank which handles the letter of credit in the country of the seller will also add its confirmation to the document, for instance will guarantee payment against presentation of correct documentation. There will be an extra charge for the buyer when he raises the letter of credit to cover this service.

4 Back to back:

This form of letter of credit is rarely used and really only applies when there is a middleman (for instance merchant) buying the goods between the exporter and importer. The merchant buys the goods from the exporter and pays for them under a confirmed, irrevocable letter of credit. To raise (get) this letter of credit he uses the importer's letter of credit in his favor as security. It means that the merchant does not have to put up the cash for the goods until he has been paid by the importer. The merchant will have added a mark-up to the price which represents his profit on the deal. It is a very good method of payment when the agent staffs importing on his own account for re-sale.

5. Revolving:

This type of letter of credit is especially useful when there are going to be multiple shipments of goods over a period of time between one supplier and one buyer. The buyer raises a letter of credit for a maximum sum that can be outstanding at any one time, say $50,000. The supplier can then ship goods up to that value and present documents to the bank for payment. Once payment has been made then the full value of the letter of credit is again available and the supplier can make a second shipment up to $50,000 in value and soon until the expiry date of the letter of credit. This type of credit is usually reserved for established customers.

The types you are most likely to come across in your dealings in overseas trade are the "irrevocable letter of credit" and the "confirmed irrevocable letter of credit".

9.3. Bills of Exchange

This is another common method of payment in overseas trade. It's a useful method of securing payment for goods supplied and was extensively used for domestic trade as well as overseas up to the end of the last century.

A bill of exchange is defined in the Bills of Exchange Act 1882 as: "An unconditional order in writing, addressed by one person to another, signed by the person giving it, requiring the person to whom it is addressed to pay on demand or at a fixed or determinable future time, a sum certain in money to, a specified person or to bearer."

Legal Basis

The U.S. law governing negotiable instruments is the Uniform Commercial Code in 49 states (Louisiana being the exception). Article 3 outlines the law of commercial paper. In cases where the UCC is silent or unclear, further interpretations can be found in numerous court decisions passed down on the subject over the years. Basically, the UCC codifies established business and banking practices and previous court decisions.

The United Kingdom's negotiable instruments law was codified in the Bills of Exchange Act of 1882. It is similar to the UCC in its major provisions and applications. Indeed, laws and practices governing negotiable instruments are similar in most countries.

However, the laws governing negotiable instruments in various countries may vary in their details. A brief review of U.S. law is given. If questions arise regarding detailed or specific issues (concerning either American laws or the laws of a specific foreign country) merchants are advised to seek legal counsel.

Conditions for Negotiability

To be a truly negotiable instrument under U.S. law:

a) A bill of exchange must be in writing and must not contain restrictive conditions.

b) The person giving it is the seller, and he must add his signature to the document.

c) The person to whom it is addressed is the buyer.

d) The buyer must accept the bill of exchange when it is presented to him by his bank, or by the supplier direct. He does this by endorsing (signing) the back of the document.

e) The buyer must pay the bill of exchange upon presentation of the document to him, or on the due date stated in the bill.

f) The value of the bill of exchange must be fixed.

g) The payment must be made to the seller or to his order through a bank, or in rare cases to the bearer of (the person holding) the bill of exchange.

The bill of exchange is dated at time of the shipment of the goods. There may therefore be a difference between the date of the bill of exchange and the date when the bill is presented to the buyer fin payment.

9.3.1 How the 'Bill of Exchange' Works

The supplier agrees payment terms with the buyer. These may be 30, 60, 90 or more days after the date of shipment of the goods, or may beat 'sight' (which means as soon as the bill of exchange is presented to the buyer or his bank). The parties agree that the terms should be secured by a bill of exchange. The supplier ships the goods to the buyer and completes the necessary shipping documents in the same way as for the letter of credit above.

9.4 Open Account

This is the simplest, but least secure, method of payment used in overseas trade. Basically the supplier ships the goods, completes the shipping documents and sends them direct to the buyer. The buyer uses the documents to release the goods from Customs and pays the supplier on the agreed date. The bank need not be involved and the process requires no special payment document. Open account is primarily used between pates that are used to trading with each other and between whom there is mutual trust.

There are six methods of making open account payments

1. By bank draft.

This is a document drawn up by the buyer's bank which guarantees payment upon presentation to the seller's bank. It is sent directly by the buyer to the seller.

2. By check

Money can be sent by international check drawn on the buyer's bank account. This is the simplest method, but of course there is the risk that the check will 'bounce'! Also, the check can take up to Three weeks to clear through the banks.

3. By mail transfer.

The buyer's bank notifies the supplier's bank by mall of the transfer of funds and the supplier's account is credited with the payment.

4. By telex or telegraph transfer.

This works in the same way as the mail transfer except that the seller's bank is notified by telex or telegraph. Hence payment is quicker but can still take up to three days.

5. By currency account.

This works in the same way as the telex or mall transfer except that payment is in a foreign currency, for instance the buyer will ask his bank to mail or telex transfer 10,000 Dollars to the supplier's bank.

The fastest methods are those using telex transfers. The others are limited to the speed of the international postal services which can take between three days and two weeks depending upon the country of posting. All the methods stated above, except the check, are arranged by the buyer's bank and hence are very secure.

6 Credit cards

Many U.S. exporters of consumer and other products (generally of low dollar value) that are sold directly to the end user accept Visa and MasterCard in payment for export sales. In international credit card transactions, merchants are normally required to deposit drafts in the currency of their country; for example, a U.S. exporter would deposit a draft in U.S. dollars. U.S. merchants may find that domestic rules and international rules governing credit card transactions differ somewhat and should contact their credit card processor for more specific information.

International credit card transactions are typically placed by phone or fax, methods that facilitate fraudulent transactions. Merchants should determine the validity of transactions and obtain proper authorizations.

9.4.1 Problems with Payment

We should mention here one or two of the problems that may arise with payment for an overseas order.

(a) Inaccurate shipping documents presented under a letter of credit

This is probably the most common payment problem in overseas trade. If ii, any ways the shipping documents presented to the advising bank (supplier's bank) under a letter of credit are incorrect, for instance disagree with the terms or wording of the letter of credit, then payment will be withheld pending further instructions from the buyer, or presentation of corrected documents. In either case this will delay payment to the supplier. That means that if one word on one document is incorrect your client may not receive his payment for the goods. For example, if on the invoice the goods are described as "induction heating equipment" but the letter of credit states "induction healing equipment" then the invoice will be rejected and payment withheld because of one letter being incorrect in the description! This example may sound improbable, but it is true, as the person presenting the documents under that particular letter of credit was the author!

There are two ways to resolve such an issue. Either the supplier can obtain corrected shipping documents and present them to his bank within the specified time limit, or he can get die buyer to accept the documents as presented. If the buyer does this then all is well and payment will be made by the bank. However, the buyer may well want to check the goods to ensure their condition is satisfactory when they arrive. He could ask the shipping agent to do this on his behalf this delay costs money in lost interest (on finds expected) if nothing else.

(b)   The Buyer delays payment (under open account terms)

This cannot arise under a letter of credit, rarely arises under a bill of exchange transaction but can arise under open account payment terms. If you are asked to intervene make sure you are tactful in your approach to the buyer. Re may have good reason for not paying and in any event you want this payment and future business from him so it might be wise not to upset him at this stage.

Try to find out what the problem is and then convey this back to your client before taking any action (for instance sending reminders) and make sure that any action you do take has to be approved by your client first.

If, however, he does not intend to pay then your client may need to take action through his credit insurers to obtain the payment due to him.

(c)   The buyer delays payment for some political reason

It occasionally happens that a country will put a hold on all payments going out of the country. This may be because of war or because the country is in financial difficulties and cannot afford to pay for its imports. It usually happens very swiftly so you can be in the middle of an overseas transaction when the block occurs meaning that your client has delivered the goods but the buyer cannot pay. In these circumstances all you can do is wait. However, your client can take some precautions to prevent this happening to him. These options follow below:

9.4.2 Credit Control

The first option is to establish his own method of credit control. This means in effect controlling how much credit a customer can have before a hold is put on any further supplies. This can have two levels of control which are usually operated simultaneously:

(1) The credit limit of a customer is set at the beginning of the relationship between supplier and customer, for instance $50,000. This means that the customer cannot at any one time owe more than $50,000. As soon as he reaches this limit shipments stop until he has paid enough invoices to bring him within the limit again. The initial amount of credit to be permitted to a buyer is usually determined by making inquires regarding his credit status. These inquiries can be made through private credit insurance companies (see below) or through banks who have departments to handle these inquiries

(2) If a customer does not pay an invoice on the due date without good reason then all shipments are 'frozen' until he pays the money.

9.4.3 Credit Insurance

There are private companies that will issue insurance to cover credit risks in both domestic and overseas trade. For the payment of a premium, usually expressed as a percentage of the order value, the insurer will cover your client's order in the event of non-payment. You should advise your client in this regard if you think there is a risk attached to any particular buyer or market.

You or your client can get an indication of the risk attached to a buyer, or a market, by asking for credit checks through the same credit insurance companies. For a fee they will offer the service of credit checking customers. This service is open to anyone who can pay the fees involved. The fee is usually in the region of two per cent of the value of the contract.

10.0 Transportation

The decision as to which method of transport to use for a particular consignment will be made by the buyer and seller, usually at the time of entering the contract. They may well refer to a shipping agent (see below) for advice and for quotations to see which method is the most suitable. Often the supplier will state the method of shipment in his original quotation as he is in the best position to decide on the method of shipment for his particular product. However, at times the advice of the commission agent may be requested.

10.1 Sea-Freight

This is the method of transporting products used most often in international trade, and upon which most mercantile law and commercial practice are based. A sea-freight shipment is one where the goods are carried by a cargo-ship or ocean-going vessel from a port in one country to a port in another. It is used a great deal to transport bulk cargoes such as wheat and copper as well as for the shipment of oil. It is also used for the shipment of most other goods where the size, or weight, of the shipment makes it either impractical or too costly to ship by other methods, for example machinery and automobiles.

How to arrange a sea-freight shipment?

The exporter will ask a shipping agent, or possibly the shipping company itself, to arrange collection of the consignment from his location. Goods traveling by sea, excluding bulk cargoes, need more careful packing than those traveling by other methods of transport because of the longer transit times and the higher risk of transit damage. Therefore, either the supplier (exporter) will have packed them for sea shipment or he will ask the shipping agent to arrange this for him. The shipping agent will book space on a vessel destined for the country of import and will notify the exporter of the name and sailing date. This information will be passed on to the buyer (importer).

The goods will be delivered to the vessel and loaded on board. At this stage the shipping document, called a "bill of lading" will be signed by the master of the vessel confirming that the goods have been loaded on board. This document, which is issued in sets of two or three originals plus the required number of copies, depending upon the letter of credit instructions, fulfills three major functions.

1) It is a receipt for the goods.
2) It is the contract of shipment between the exporter and the shipping line.
3) It is a document of title to the goods, for instance whoever has the original bills of lading can obtain the goods at the port of destination.

These bills of lading are sent to the importer either directly or, if certain payment terms apply to the contract, through the banks so that the importer can clear the goods through Customs and take ownership at the port of destination.

The originals and copies of the bill of lading are usually distributed as follows:

- All of the originals should go to the shipper (supplier) unless he has stated otherwise, for instance he may have asked for one original to go with the vessel so that the consignee (the person receiving the goods, for instance the importer) can clear the goods quickly through Customs upon their arrival at the port of destination, and take possession of them. Each original bill of lading is a valid title (that is, a legal claim to ownership) to the goods so the first person to present a bill of lading to the master of the vessel will gain possession of the goods. The reason for issuing more than one original is partly historical in that should one original get lost in transit there will still be others to give title to the goods.

- Copies of the originals are not signed by the master and are not documents of title to the goods. They are usually distributed as follows:
  - One is retained by the shipping line.
  - One is retained by the shipping agent, if one has been used.
  - One is given to the consignee (importer).
  - One is retained by the shipper (exporter).
  - One is retained by the bank, if one has been involved.

Sea -freight shipment has the following advantages.

- It is usually cheaper than other methods of shipment.
- Sea shipments can be larger and heavier than other shipments.
- It is ideally suited for the movement of bulk cargoes.

However, it also has the following disadvantages

- It is slower than most other forms of transport.
- There is an increased risk of damage or loss at sea and therefore more secure, and hence expensive, packing must be used to protect the goods.
- It is less flexible in that loading and off-loading are restricted to deep water harbors.

10.2 Air-Freight

This is an increasingly popular method of shipment. It lends itself extremely well to smaller, higher-value consignments where quick delivery is important. However, nowadays quite large loads can be transported on modem freighter aircraft and size and weight have become less of a restriction.

How to arrange an air-freight shipment

The supplier (exporter) will ask a shipping agent, or possibly the airline directly, to arrange collection of the goods from his location. Goods traveling by air generally need less packing than cargoes traveling by sea. Such packing as is required will be carried out either by the exporter or by the shipping agent. The agent will coiled the goods from the exporter and will book them on to the next available aircraft flying to the country of destination. The agent will provide the exporter with an 'air waybill' number, flight number and date of shipment. This information will be passed onto the importer by the exporter.

The goods will be loaded on to the aircraft and the 'air waybill' will be signed and dated by the airline before being passed back to the shipping agent. This document is both a receipt for the goods and the evidence of shipment. It is not; however, a document of title to the goods as is the case with a sea-freight 'bill of lading'. Whoever the goods have been consigned to at destination has title to the goods.

The signed, original air waybill will be sent to the importer either directly or, if certain payment terms apply to the contract, through the banks so that the importer can clear the goods through Customs and take ownership at the airport of destination.

Copies will be retained by the airline, shipping agent (if used), exporter, bank (if used) and consignee (importer).

Air-freight shipment has the following advantages

- It is faster than sea-freight.

- It is more flexible because of the location of airports, which can be inland or coastal.
- It is ideally suited for smaller, urgent, high-value or perishable cargoes.
- It is easier to arrange and involves less paperwork.
- The goods are less likely to be damaged in transit.
- Through the method of grouping' or 'consolidating' lots of small air-freight shipments into larger ones you can get the benefits of cheaper freight rates.

However, it also has the following disadvantages.

- The weight and size of the shipment are limited by the size of aircraft carrying the goods, especially if it is a passenger aircraft, which only carries cargo in small holds.
- It tends to be more expensive than sea-freight, although this needs to be checked for each shipment as sometimes it can prove cheaper, especially for smaller shipments.
- It is not as flexible as road transport.

10.3 Road Transport

Road transport is probably the most flexible and easiest method of international shipping with the possible exception of postal shipment (see below). However, problems can arise if the journey involves crossing the sea.

The goods are collected from the exporter's door and are delivered to the importer's door and handling in between is only necessary if the goods are to be grouped with other consignments going to the same country of destination. If the consignment is a 'full load' (for instance enough to fill up one vehicle) then the goods will not be handled at all while in transit. Also road transport can, within reason, handle any cargo from one small package to a 20,000 lbs piece of machinery. Low-value bulk cargoes, such as grain or milk, and high-value individual items, such as cars or computers, can all be catered for.

How to arrange a road shipment?

The exporter will again use the services of a shipping agent, one who specializes in road haulage. The goods will be suitably packed to travel by road (about the same amount of packing as required for airfreight shipment), and will then be collected directly from the exporter's location, If the consignment is a full load then the collecting vehicle will take the goods all the way to the destination. If the goods are only a part load, then they will be 'grouped' with other consignments going to the same country of destination. That way the vehicle that eventually leaves will have become a full load with consequent savings in freight costs for all the exporters involved.

The document given to the exporter as a receipt for the goods, and evidence of shipment, is called a "consignment note". Again it is not a document of title to the goods. Title belongs to the person to whom the goods are consigned at destination. The consignment note will be sent by the exporter to the importer either directly or, if certain payment terms apply to the contract, through the banks so that the importer can clear the goods through Customs and take ownership. Usually copies of this document are retained by the exporter, the forwarding (shipping) agent, the haulage company; the bank (if one is involved) and the consignee (importer) will receive the original.

Road shipment has the following advantages:

- It is very flexible, not being restricted to specific points of loading and off-loading.

- It is less expensive than air-freight and sometimes than sea-freight
- It is reasonably fast, especially when compared with sea-freight.
- It is adaptable to all types of cargo.
- It is easy to arrange.
- The goods are less likely to be damaged in transit.

However, it also has the following disadvantages:

- It is somewhat slower than air-freight.
- It is more expensive than sea-freight.
- It cannot be used for shipment to countries that are separated by oceans.

10.4 Couriers

Couriers carry urgent documents and goods using a number of different methods of transport. For example, company 'A' wants an urgent document sent from its offices in New York to a customer's location in Toronto, Canada. It calls the courier company and lists its requirements. The courier company collects the document from company 'A' (usually on the same day) and gives the company a receipt for the package. The package is then sorted, along with all the other packages received that day, into destinations. All the items for Toronto are loaded on to a truck and are taken to the airport for the flight to Toronto. When the packages arrive at Toronto they are again sorted, this time into postal districts, and are delivered to their destinations by van. The operation is then complete.

Couriers have the following advantages:

- They are very fast.

- They are door-to-door.
- They are very flexible.
- They are ideal for moving urgently required documents and small packages.

However, they also have the ff1/owing disadvantages:

- There are restrictions on the size or weight of package that can be carried.
- They are quite expensive compared with other forms of transport.

10.5 Postal Shipment

Postal shipment is usually by far the easiest, quickest and cheapest method of international shipment for small packages. However, it has serious limitations with regard to both size and weight of individual packages. Within these limitations however it is a very effective method of shipment. It is suitable for all types of goods that fall within the weight and size limits.

How to make a postal shipment?

To arrange a postal shipment the exporter does not need the services of a shipping agent, shipment can be arranged directly with the Post Office. He does need to ensure that the goods are well packed in suitable containers before posting. He then completes a Customs form (obtained from the Post Office), and attaches a copy of his invoice and takes the parcel to his nearest Post Office. (If he is a regular user then the Post Office may well arrange collection facilities from his location.) The Post Office gives him a postal receipt and ships the goods to the location of the importer.

The postal receipt will be passed to the importer by the exporter in the same way as stated above for other methods of shipment. The postal receipt is just a receipt, it is not a document of title to the goods.

When goods are imported by post they must pass through Customs in the same way as goods arriving by other methods of shipment. Normally the arrival of the goods is notified to the consignee (importer) by the Post Office, International Section. The form that is used for notification will give details of the consignment and will contain a declaration that must be signed by the importer. The goods will clear Customs and will be mailed directly to the importer. Free gifts and "samples" are normally excluded from this procedure.

Postal shipment has the following advantages:

- it is much cheaper than other methods of international shipment.
- The single charge for the stamp is all that needs to be paid for shipment (except for Customs charges on importation, if applicable).
- It is fast if the airmail facility is used. Surface mail takes the same transit time as sea-freight.
- It is easy to arrange as no shipping agent need be involved.
- It is a door-to-door service, hence total flexibility.
- It is global in availability - it can be used throughout the world - there are postal services in nearly every country in the world.

However, it also has the following disadvantages.

- Weight restrictions per parcel, vehicle can be overcome in part by shipping multiple parcels.
- Size restrictions per parcel.

10.6 Export Packaging

Generally speaking goods being exported require more careful and substantial packing than those for domestic shipment. This is for a number of reasons:

* The longer distances involved.

* The more frequent handling of the consignment.

* The increased risk of shock damage while in transit.

* The changes in temperature and humidity.

* The risk of water penetration.

* The increased risk of theft.

Therefore, before the exporter ships the consignment he will need to have the goods suitably packed for the method of shipment and destination involved. The supplier can either do this packing himself at his location or employ the services of a specialist packing company. Many shipping agents offer export packing services to their customers.

10.7 Shipping Marks

When the goods have been suitably packed into their outer containers they will need to be marked carefully to avoid loss or damage during transit. Shipping marks are placed on packages for three main reasons:

1. Identity

To identify the package so that it can be easily traced back to the supplier or the recipient. For example, a crate destined for India by sea-freight may be marked as follows:

BOMBAY FOUNDRY

BOMBAY

ORDER 1000/92

SUPPLIER: ABC MACHINE TOOLS, NEW-YORK

2. Protection

To prevent damage occurring. For example, the crate mentioned above should be kept upright at all times, therefore the marking will be:

III

THIS WAY UP

3. Safety

Packages are marked for safety reasons. To use the above example again, perhaps the machine tools have light oil in their system. The warning might read as follows:

WARNING - IRRITANT

DO NOT TIP OR SPILL

10.8 Container Traffic

Much of the sea-freight traffic of today (and some air-freight and road freight) is shipped in containers. You have probably seen them being carried by trucks, especially on the freeway. They are usually 6 meters (20 feet) or 12 meters (40 feet) in length, although there are variations. Their other dimensions are usually 2.5 meters (8 feet) x 2.5 meters (8 feet).

The advantages of packing goods in containers are as follows:

- Less conventional packing needs to be used.
- The containers are designed for more than one method of transport (multi-modal). This means that they can be loaded onto ships, trucks or trains easily and quickly.
- More cargo can be stored into a given space. The carrying vessels are designed for maximum storage capability and can carry many times the cargo that could be carried by conventional sea-freight vessels of the same size,
- Docks are designed and equipped for rapid turn-around of vessels.
- There are few differences in procedures and documentation between containerized traffic and conventional sea-freight.
- Special containers can be used to transport goods requiring a controlled environment, for instance frozen food

10.9 Commercial Invoice

The invoice is essential to every overseas shipment. Goods cannot pass through Customs without a copy Invoice. This document should show the following information:

- Name and address of supplier.
- Name and address of buyer and country of destination.
- The invoice should be numbered and dated.
- The goods should be detailed, showing price and total value.
- Any ancillary (extra) charges such as freight and insurance should be shown. The payment terms should be given, for instance Irrevocable Letter of Credit
- The method of shipment, for instance air-freight
- The size and weight of the goods should be shown.
- The delivery terms should be given, for instance FOB Chicago.

- The invoice needs to be signed.

The document must be prepared by the exporter at time of shipment. At least one copy will be required by Customs. The original should be sent to the importer at time of shipment either directly or through banks if certain payment terms apply. One copy always accompanies the goods.

10.10 Consular Invoice

This document is necessary when you are exporting to certain countries as evidence of origin of the goods and value. It is a legal requirement of some countries. It is either a special document issued by the Consulate of die country concerned or a special stamp put on a normal copy of the commercial invoice.

You can find out if a consular invoice is necessary by contacting a Department of commerce or a shipping agent; either body will assist you in this regard. The purpose of the document is to prove the country of origin of the goods and to certify that the invoice is correct and does not conflict with any regulations in the country of import. It must be prepared by the exporter at the time of shipment. One copy will be retained by the consulate or embassy concerned. One copy should accompany the shipment of the goods. The original should be sent to the importer at time of shipment either directly or through the bank. The shipping agent will often arrange consular legalization for the exporter.

10.11 Proforma Invoice

This document has two main purposes in overseas trade:

1. It is used to obtain payment in advance of shipment. If the seller wants payment in advance from a buyer then he may need to

provide a proforma invoice prior to the shipment of the goods. This document shows all the same information as a normal commercial invoice.

2. A proforma invoice is issued so that the buyer can raise a letter of creditor obtain permission to transfer money abroad. In some countries such a document is essential to get this permission. The buyer will know if he needs a proforma invoice for this purpose.

The document must be prepared by the exporter before shipment takes place.

10.12 Certificate of Origin

Certificates of origin are issued by chambers of commerce. It is evidence of the country of origin of the goods. It is an official document which can be bought from the Department of commerce in sets. If you are a member of the chamber then the fee for certification of these documents is reduced. The exporter or his shipping agent completes the document and sends it to the Department of commerce for stamping and signing.

Sometimes these certificates need to be stamped by the Consulate of the country of destination. There is an additional fee for providing this service. You can find out the Department of commerce or the relevant embassy. This certificate is not needed for all countries. Your Department of commerce or a shipping agent will be able to advise you on which countries require this document.

The information given in the certificate of origin is as follows

- Name and address of exporter

- Name and address of importer

- Description of goods

- Number of units

- Weight of the goods

- Country of origin of the goods (even Lf that is not the country of departure). The Department of commerce relies upon the honesty of the exporter in this regard as they have no way of checking the validity of the information contained in the document.

- Method of shipment

- It should be signed and dated

The document should be prepared at the time of shipment. A copy of the document should accompany the shipment. The original should be sent to the importer at the time of shipment either directly or through the bank. Similar documents are issued by the chambers of commerce in other countries for their exporters and these fulfill the same function.

10.13 Insurance Policy/Certificate

This is an essential document in an overseas contract. Whoever is responsible for arranging insurance for the goods while in transit is also responsible for obtaining either a specific insurance policy to cover the goods or an insurance certificate if the exporter has a general policy with the insurance company. It is the evidence of the contract of insurance.

Freight insurance is the general name for the insurance of goods while in transit. The name implies sea-freight as the method of shipment but in fact the same term covers all methods of shipment and storage of goods.

The shipping agent will often arrange insurance on behalf of either the supplier or the buyer and will charge a fee for thus service along with the insurance premium. However, insurance can be arranged directly with a freight insurance company. Such companies are often listed in the phone book or a shipping agent will be able to recommend one.

Freight insurance can, and often does, cover more than just the transportation of the goods. It will cover for loss, theft, damage and pilferage while in transit as well as while in storage and during inland transportation to and from the carrying vessel or aircraft,

Whoever arranges such insurance should send a copy of the policy or certificate to the other party in the transaction, preferably at the time of shipment. The value of the goods for insurance purposes is equal to their fill CIF value plus 10% to cover for additional costs in making the claim for loss.

10.14 Import License

This document is sometimes required for goods entering the country of destination. It is issued by the relevant government department and must be obtained by the importer before the goods are shipped from the country of export. It is the importers responsibility to obtain the document if required and to notify the exporter of its particulars.

It is used as a control mechanism for regulating imports. This may be a means of restricting the importation of dangerous goods such as some chemicals. Since a country loses its currency when it is used to pay for imports, import licenses are also a way of controlling the amount of currency leaving the country.

10.15 Movement Certificate

This document is required if the goods are moving within the European Community (EC). The certificate is prepared by the exporter, is endorsed by Customs in the country of export and is stamped again each time the goods cross a national border. It is evidence that goods are in "flee circulation" within the EC. That means that all import duties have been paid (if applicable), or that the goods are of EC origin and now enjoy duty-free status.

Copies of this document can be obtained from Customs office or a shipping agent.

10.16 Export License

This document is the opposite of the import license mentioned above. It is issued by the relevant government department and covers certain restricted goods. It must be obtained by the exporter before the goods are shipped from the country of export. It is the exporter's responsibility to obtain this document if required and to pass it to Customs at the time of shipment.

It is used as a control mechanism for regulating exports. This may be a means of controlling the export of restricted articles such as some chemicals or the export of certain technology.

10.17 Customs Export/Import Documents

Every import movement and every export movement has to have a Customs document showing details of the goods and their movement. This applies to all countries. Nowadays the shipping agent usually prepares these documents on behalf of the exporter or importer but great care must be taken in their completion as there are severe penalties for incorrect Customs entries.

The document will show details such as description of goods, value and possibly weight, destination, place of export, name and address of exporter, the Customs tariff number applicable for the category of goods. This form will be signed and dated by the exporter/importer, or in some cases it can be done by the agent providing he has written authority to do so from the importer or exporter.

The document is prepared at the time of shipment but must be presented to and signed and stamped by Customs before shipment takes place or in the case of importation before the goods are released to the consignee (importer).

10.18 Quality Certificate

This document is sometimes required for goods when the buyer has seen only a sample of the items and wants confirmation that the total shipment agrees with the specification of the sample. Often it is used simply as a way of giving the buyer a written guarantee of quality for the merchandise he is purchasing. It is issued by the supplier and confirms that the goods conform to specification in the sales contract.

10.19 Customs Clearance

Above we have looked at international shipping methods. Let us now consider what happens to the goods when they arrive at the country of destination.

First, they have to be cleared through Customs. That means that the Customs authority of the country of import will want to see the documents that relate to the shipment. They may also want physically to examine the goods, which they are entitled to do, but this is rare nowadays. The documents they will want to see are.

(a)   The commercial invoice - giving details of the goods, their price and the name and address of the buyer of those goods. They will want to keep one copy of the invoice.

(b)   The customs entry form.

(c)   Any required import license.

(d)   The transport document. This could be a bill of lading, airway bill, consignment note or postal receipt depending upon the method of shipment.

(e)   A certificate of origin - stating the country of origin of the goods may also be required. Department of commerce can advise exporters upon which countries need such certificates.

The above documents will have been sent to the importer by the exporter at the time of shipment. The shipping agent or carrier will have notified the importer of the arrival of the goods and will inform him of the required documents and procedures.

Once Customs have seen these documents and have accepted them as correct they will charge the importer any relevant import duty and taxes. Once this is paid the goods will be released This warehouse ,nay belong to a shipping line, airline or even a shipping agent, but goods cannot be moved out of it until Customs have passed the documentation. This process normally takes one or two days if the documents are correct. The goods, once passed by Customs, are free to be delivered to the importer (consignee). It is the importer's responsibility to clear the goods through Customs, not the commission agent's. Many importers will use the services of a shipping agent to carry out this task but nonetheless the importer is responsible for the actions of the shipping agent in the eyes of Customs.

10.20 The Role of the Shipping Agent

The shipping agent may also be referred to as:

- Freight forwarder
- Forwarding agent
- Clearance agent

However, despite this varying descriptions, these people perform the same function, for instance they assist exporters and importers with the international movement of goods.

10.20.1 Selecting a Shipping Agent

(a) Draw up a list of between three and six shipping agents. You will find them listed in Yellow Pages as stated above or you can contact the Institute of Freight Forwarders, which can provide a list of shipping agents registered with them.

(b) Phone, or write, to these agents asking for their freight rates and charges tariff

(c) Once you have received their tariffs, which will normally be accompanied by brochures detailing their services and the name of the representative who will be your contact, compare the costs and service levels and decide upon a shortlist of the most promising agents.

(d) Phone the contacts for each of the agents you are interested in and ask for an appointment to meet and discuss your requirements more carefully. Remember that the published tariffs are often just a starting point; much more favorable rates can often be negotiated between shipper (exporter) and agent.

(e) Before the meeting prepare a note of the questions you need to ask, For example:

- Are all the charges listed in the tariff
- What discount on those rates can they offer?
- What transit times are involved?
- Can they offer packing facilities?
- Can they prepare consular and customs documents for you? If so, at what cost?
- Will they offer you credit facilities?

(f) The meeting itself is usually cordial as shipping agent representatives are a friendly group of individuals and often conversations with them take several hours because you spend about an hour discussing everything under the sun except shipping when you first meet!

(g) The meeting is a negotiation to find the best level of service and cost structure for your requirement, and to give the agent a price that will cover his costs and make him a reasonable profit. You know the starting point - the tariff already provided - so that is the most that you will have to pay. From now on it can only get better!

(h) Once the negotiation is complete you should ask the agent to confirm the discussion points in writing so that you are both sure in your understanding of what has been discussed and decided.

(i) When you have met and negotiated with the short listed agents you should be in a position to decide between them and to appoint one of them as your agent. It is a good idea to have them on a trial basis for a month or two at first just to see that they live up to their promises. At the end of the trial period you can confirm the position either in writing or just verbally. There is seldom a binding, written agreement between shipper and shipping agent.

11.0 World Markets

11.1 Trade in North America

Industries

One of the great advantages of trade with North America is that English is the main language both spoken and used in commerce. Exceptions to this are parts of Canada, where French is the main language, and again in some of the south-western states of the US, where Spanish is commonly spoken.

If you have the opportunity to travel within Canada you will experience the vast consumer market that exists there and this will give you some indication of the enormous trading opportunities that exist.

Major products entering international trade with North America are machinery, electrical goods, medicines, motor vehicles, clothing, chemicals and foodstuffs.

Payment terms

Open account or bill of exchange terms are generally used when trading with this region.

Transport

Sea-freight, air-freight and postal shipment are the most commonly used forms of transportation.

Language

English is the principal language of the region. French and Spanish, however, are important in certain territories.

11.2 Trade in South America

Industries

The major trading block amongst these nations is LAFTA, the Latin America Free Trade Area. There are a number of restrictions on imports into these countries to encourage and protect domestic production. This takes the form of quantity restrictions (quotas), high import duty rates and complete bans on certain goods. Having said this there are moves to open up these markets to European manufacturers and existing opportunities make it a worthwhile market to tackle.

Products entering international trade with South America include: meat products, cereals, coffee, foodstuffs, wool, timber, copper, tin, cotton, chemicals, machinery, electrical goods and vehicles.

Payment terms

"Irrevocable letter of credit" terms are the norm for this region and care must be taken when exporting to make sure that the buyer has the relevant import license.

Transport

Sea-freight, air-freight and postal shipment are the usual methods of transport.

Language

English is understood in the commercial sector; however Spanish is the main language, with Portuguese being spoken in Brazil.

11.3 Trade in the Caribbean

Industries

Trade generally involves the export of natural products and craft goods from the Caribbean and the import of consumer and light industrial goods in return. The products traded include foodstuffs, bananas, sugar, coffee, cocoa, cotton, clothing, chemicals, machinery, electrical goods and vehicles.

Payment terms

"Irrevocable letter of credit" is to be recommended for trade in this region. Bills of exchange are acceptable once the relationship is established.

Transport

Sea-freight and air-freight are the normal methods of transport. Postal shipment can be slow,

Language

English is widely spoken and understood French and Spanish are also common in this region.

11.4 Trade in Western Europe

Industries

Thousands of products enter trade between the highly industrialized nations of Western Europe. We obviously cannot list each one in a manual of this nature. What we can do is to tell you the client industries involved m international trade within Western Europe. Let us first consider the natural resources of the region that enter international trade These include: Coal, natural gas, petroleum, fertilizers, timber, cereals, beverages, vegetables, fruits, vegetable oils, meat, dairy produce, fish and seafood's, wine in addition to these natural products we have the manufacturing industries and their products: Machinery, tools, textiles, electrical engineering, high-tech, computers, agricultural, automobiles, aircraft, mining, precision instruments, telecommunications, information technology, watches and clocks, white goods (refrigerators, ovens and washing machines), chemicals.

As can be seen from this list, most products are actively being traded within Western Europe. In addition to this there are the products that are imported from outside of the area, both essential raw materials and a wide range of industrial and consumer products. These goods come from all over the world, especially the Far East and North America.

Here are a few specific ideas that you can follow up. Some of the Southern European countries can offer very cheap supplies of products that are ideal for importation. For example, Portugal is a good source of linen products, (towels and bed linen), clothes, shoes and industrial components This applies also to Greece, Spain and Turkey, although as the standard of living in these countries continues to rise at exceptional rates the price differences are becoming less significant. From an exporter's point of view all of the countries of Western Europe are worthwhile markets. However, you may need to be competitive on pricing as there are usually a number of suppliers seeking the customer's business.

Payment terms

Throughout Western Europe open account payment terms are predominant. In some cases bills of exchange maybe used to safeguard payment

Transport

The most common forms of transportation used for goods moving within Western Europe are road transport, air-freight and postal shipment. Within the continent itself barge transport is commonly used owing to the extensive river network.

Language

English is widely understood throughout the region. French, German, Spanish and Italian are also common.

11.5 Trade in Eastern Europe

Industries

The Eastern European countries are strong markets for goods produced in the West, both industrial and consumer goods. The major industries of the region are timber, engineering, textiles, chemicals, agriculture, coal, metals.

Payment terms

The payment terms used for trade with Eastern Europe is usually "irrevocable Letter of Credit". Credit insurance cover is recommended when supplying goods to Eastern Europe. Payment should always be requested in sterling rather than the domestic currency of the importer to avoid exchange rate differences.

Transport

Road transport and air-freight are the two most common methods. Rail and canal are also important within Eastern Europe. Sea-freight to the Russian ports is also common.

Language

English is widely understood in the commercial sphere. Russian, German and the Slavic languages are commonly used.

11.6 Trade in the Middle East

Industries

Politically this region of the world has been unstable over the past decade, making trade difficult at times. Disastrous conflicts in Lebanon, Iran and Iraq have almost halted trade between these countries and the rest of the world. Hopefully this situation will improve and strong trading links will soon once again be forged.

Despite this instability most trade goods, both industrial and consumer, flow into the Middle East and opportunities for successful trade are plentiful. However, there are generally some precautions necessary for secure trading with this region.

Payment terms

Until you have established an on-going trading relationship with a buyer, it is best to trade on "confirmed, irrevocable Letter of Credit" payment terms.

Transport.

You generally need legalized invoices and certificates of origin for goods exported to Middle East countries so check with a Department of commerce, shipping agent or with the embassy concerned before making shipment. In addition, in some of these countries, notably the Arab countries, there are restrictions on the import of goods of Israeli origin and goods shipped on Israeli vessels or aircraft. You may also be refused entry to some of these countries if you have an Israeli passport. Sea-freight, road transport, and airfreight are all common methods of shipment used to the Middle East. Postal shipment is less commonly used because of the haphazard nature of the postal services in some of these countries.

Language English and French are widely understood throughout the region. Hebrew, Arabic and Farsi are also common languages.

11.7 Trade in Asia

Industries

Nearly every type product that enters world trade is produced in the Far East. However, certain industries are more prominent than others, for example:

Natural resources

Rice, tea, cotton, timber, bamboo, leather, spices, silk, seafood.

Manufacturing

Clothing, toys, giftware, jewelry, textiles, electrical goods, computers, bicycles, chinaware.

Payment Terms

The usual payment terms for the region are "confirmed, irrevocable letter of credit". Once a trading relationship has been achieved then payment by bill of exchange may be introduced.

Transport

The most commonly used methods of transport for the Far East are sea-freight, air-freight, sea/air shipment (combining both sea and air transport) and post.

Language

Once again English is widely understood in the commercial community. However, the most common languages are Chinese (Mandarin), Japanese and Hindi-Urdu.

11.8 Trade in Australia

Industries

This region is wealthy in natural resources and is developing important manufacturing industries, the main natural resources are: wool, mutton, minerals, chemicals, butter and fruit. Exports are predominantly agricultural. Imports cover the whole range of consumer and industrial goods, including machinery, electrical goods, petroleum products, food and chemicals.

Payment terms

Because of the links with the old British Empire, and more recently the Commonwealth, open account and bill of exchange payment is fairly commonplace in trade with Australia. Credit insurance is to be recommended however before trading commences.

Transport

The most common methods of transportation used are sea-freight, air-freight and postal shipment.

Language

The predominant language used in the region is English.

11.9 Trade in Africa

Industries

The continent is wealthy in minerals and natural resources. For example: copper, gold, diamonds, bananas, citrus fruits. Manufacturing industry is very limited and is concentrated in a few of the African countries such as Kenya, South Africa and Zimbabwe. Most of the other emerging nations are trying hard to industrialize rather than be dependent upon imported goods. The major import items are food, raw materials, chemicals, machinery, petroleum products, textiles and vehicles.

Payment terms

Confirmed, irrevocable letter of credit" is to be recommended mall cases along with credit insurance cover for each order.

Transport

The most common forms of transport used in trade with this region are sea-freight and air-freight. Postal shipment can be hazardous because of the unreliable nature of many of the postal services in the region.

Language

English is widely understood within the region owing to the former colonization of many areas of the continent. French and Portuguese are also understood in some areas for the same reason. Swahili is also commonly spoken.

12.0 Profit Planning

12.1 Computer Equipment - Export

Computer equipment covers a considerable range of products, for example personal computers parts, modem, printers, keyboards, software (programs) and so on. You have to firstly decide which items you are going to sell. Research of the product is essential as you will be expected to have at least a basic knowledge of computers - it is a highly technical field.

While you are researching the products, start with the search for a client you will need to contact a number of domestic suppliers to see if they are interested in exporting their products, and, if so, to which export markets. At least ten suppliers should be contacted so that you can compare the replies you receive.

These suppliers may want further information from you. Provide this as quickly as possible so that you appear efficient and enthusiastic. Providing you appear to know what you are doing you may be offered an agency agreement with one of these suppliers. Commission rates vary but you would expect to achieve between 5 and 12 per cent commission.

Having obtained your agency you now need to find your buyers. You firstly have to ask yourself:

Which is the best way to market this product? Who are you trying to reach?
Where computer products are involved, you 'nay be trying to sell into one of the distribution channels or you may be trying to reach the end user, or indeed both. If you were marketing PCs (personal computers) or printers then your activity would probably be directed towards

the distributors or dealers, leaving them to arrange the smaller end user sales. If, however, you were selling software you may sell direct to the end user via mail-order or internet marketing because the product lends itself to that method of distribution. Your research will need to highlight the distribution channels that are most effective in the market concerned.

Secondly, you need to consider which markets to tackle. The computer industry is not confined to the industrialized countries; every nation now has some requirement for computer technology. In fact, some of the developing nations have a greater requirement because they are just starting.

When you have decided both which sales channel(s) and which market(s) to approach you need to list as many potential buyers as possible from all available research sources. This is your basic prospect list which you should continually add to from further research. A contact letter should be sent to each of these prospects with details of your product range.

In reply to these letters you may receive further requests for information which again should be answered promptly. You may also receive specific orders. These should be passed back to your client as quickly as possible making sure that you keep a copy for your files. You should be prepared, however, to have to follow up these initial contact letters with the proper correspondence, or even phone calls if required, to elicit an order - they rarely fall into your hands!

Let us assume that you have received an official order - what do you do now? Well, as mentioned above, you need to pass the original back to your client so that he can accept the order and make preparations for production and delivery. But there are also a number of things you should check to make sure there are no problems with the order, and also so that you can assist your client if required. These are:

- Is the order correct with regard to prices, payment terms, delivery method and so on?
- Is all export licenses necessary for these goods? If so, has it been applied for?
- Are there any special packing requirements for these technical products?
- Is an import license required in the country of destination? If so, has it been applied for by the buyer?
- Is a letter of credit required? If so, has it been raised by the buyer? Has it been received by your client? Is it correct in every regard? If not, has that been communicated to the buyer?
- What is the method of shipment? Has space been booked on the vessel or aircraft?

Take an interest in these issues even if the exporter, your client, is happy to deal with all of it himself -which is often the case. The more you can learn at this stage the better.

After the goods are ready and have been shipped, again there are things to be checked.
- Has the shipping documents been received by the exporter?
- If a letter of credit is involved, have the documents been checked for accuracy? Have they been presented to the bank?
- Have the goods arrived safely in the country of destination?
- Has your client been paid by the buyer?
- Have you been paid your commission?
- Is there any follow-up action required with the buyer?

At this stage the order should be complete and you will have been paid and you are ready for the next!

12.2 Computer Equipment - Import

This is really the above situation in reverse. You are looking for an overseas client and domestic buyers. The same basic principles apply as mentioned above. However, there are new considerations with regard to marketing of the product and finding your buyers.

If you are going to import this type of equipment you will need to look for countries that produce good quality, competitively priced products. There are a number of these, for example Japan, Korea, Malaysia, Germany and France. By carrying out your research you will find the names of a range of suppliers in these countries. These are your prospective clients.

When you have beet, appointed as an agent you need to decide upon the best method of marketing the product in your ova, country The first thing to remember is that the computer industry is quite a sophisticated market and that you need to adapt your approach accordingly. Purchase or borrow some good quality computer magazines and study these to see how others are tackling marketing their products. A great deal of computer equipment is sold through distributors and dealers because these offer add-on benefits such as installation services, leasing facilities and on-site training. However, there is also a large direct sale market where consumers buy direct from the manufacturer or agent through or web marketing.

Your buyers can be broken down into three types:

- Corporations - for instance large companies that purchase in bulk for their own use

- Distribution channels - for instance companies that buy from you to on-sell to others.

- End-users - for instance the person who wants to purchase and use the computer.

These are some additional considerations to be taken into account with the importation of computer equipment:

- Is an import license necessary for these goods?

- Is the power supply correct for the domestic market?

- Is the imported equipment compatible with existing domestic equipment?

- How will the equipment be shipped? Will it be adequately protected for shipment?

- What will the import duty rate be, if any is applicable?

- How will the goods be paid for? If a letter of credit is involved, has this been raised by the buyer? Is it correct?

Again it is useful for you to take an interest in these areas even if the buyer and seller handle the transaction directly.

For further information concerning computer equipment contact the major suppliers of both hardware and software requesting copies of their promotional material.

12.3 Spices, Sauces and Other Food Ingredients - Export

These are popular items in international trade because of the huge markets for them, the repetitive purchasing of such products, and the relatively high value to weight ratio. There are, however, special considerations with such products.

Firstly, the suppliers of such items are highly specialized and you may need to do more research to discover them. On the other hand there are many small, family businesses in this market that have not yet tackled the export markets of the world and would appreciate the assistance of a good export agent. Many of these companies are great fun to work with and some of their products are delicious - an added incentive when marketing the product you will need to adapt your approach to the type of buyer you are seeking. For example:

*   Import agent - if you are going to supply the product to an import agent based in the buyer's country that will break down the product from bulk to smaller retail packs then you will need to specifically target these people.

*   Catering outlets - if you are going to supply the more widespread market of retailers and caterers then you will use more general methods of marketing, for instance mail-shots.

*   Food manufacturers - if you are going to supply to the food processing industry then you will again be very specific in your marketing because each order could be significant in both size and value. A mall-shot in this instance is unlikely to be as effective as individual, specific contacts

The special considerations when exporting these products are as follows:

- Food products are subject to health and packaging regulations which must be complied with
- Export licenses may be required for certain goods in this category.
- Special care must be taken when preparing the goods for overseas shipment to protect them from moisture damage, condensation and extremes of temperature as well as the normal risks of goods in transit, for instance theft and handling damage.

- Many of these products have a shelf life, for instance a period after which they are unfit for human consumption. This must be borne in mind when shipping them overseas.
- Specialist packers and shippers are often best for handling this type of cargo.
- Many of the importing countries have strong regulations covering the importation of these products, especially with regard to quality and packaging.

It is always best to check very carefully with both seller and buyer where these products are concerned to ensure that all the necessary steps have been taken for the successful overseas shipment.

Commission rates vary but are generally smaller than with industrial equipment, say 7.5%. Most countries of the world import a selection of these products.

12.4 Engineering Equipment - Export

Engineering equipment covers a wide diversity of products including mechanical and electrical equipment for industrial use, tools, boilers, testing equipment etc. This is an area where agents are used extensively, especially specialist agents concentrating upon certain industries.

Marketing these products is somewhat different from marketing consumer products
Generally speaking these products are supplied directly by the manufacturer to the end-user. This happens for a number of reasons:

- The equipment is often custom built to meet the particular requirements of the buyer.
- The technical complexity of the product may require on-site training for the

operators.

- The production time required for these products can be considerable, perhaps months.
- The payment terms may involve payment in stages made at certain points, for example: 10% on order, 80 % on shipment and 10% on installation.

The agent is particularly useful in these circumstances, acting as the essential link between seller and buyer.

The special considerations applying to export agents in this sphere are as follows:

- A higher degree of technical knowledge is often expected by the client - you will need to study the product and the industry concerned if you are going to be successful in this area.
- The products are often major, capital items consisting of high-value, single sales to a customer not the repetitive sales you could expect with many other products
- After-sales service may be expected of the agent.
- Export licenses may be required for certain goods going to certain destinations.
- Heavy lift equipment, special packaging and specialized transport vehicles may all be required for these goods.
- Specialized payment terms may be involved. Often payment terms for these products can be spread over a long period.
- Guarantees and warranties may be required for the products.

These products offer a tremendous opportunity for the export agent but you may need to work harder to earn your commission. Commission rates vary but between 3% and 10%

would be the norm. (For example, a piece of machinery costing FOB $ 92,000 would bring you in average $ 6000 commission.) Most of this type of equipment goes to markets in the industrialized nations. However, as developing nations build up their own domestic engineering industries the demand for this type of equipment will continue to grow, especially in the Eastern European market.

12.5 Engineering Equipment - Import

A great deal of this type of equipment is imported by most nations, both industrialized and developing. No one nation is self-sufficient in this area. The primary suppliers are, of course, the industrialized nations, especially Western Europe and Japan.

Where the import agent is concerned much of the above information regarding exporting will be applicable as in the case of the export agent with the following additional considerations:

- Import licenses may be required.
- The buyer may have to arrange special payment terms with security.
- Special handling and transport facilities may be needed by the buyer when the goods arrive.
- Installation, servicing and other after-sales services may be required of the agent although a higher commission rate is applied in these cases.

Despite these complications this is a very worthwhile area of exploration for the agent.

12.6 Clothing - Export

This is another area that is popular with agents. It is a relatively easy product to understand, everyone in the world is a potential buyer and the product is usually a repeat purchase. Those are three good reasons for entering this area of trade.

When marketing this product you need to consider the channels that are available to you:

- Import agent - these will be bulk supplies that will then be broken down into smaller wholesale or retail orders by the import agent based in the buyer's country.
- Wholesalers - you could supply bulk orders to a wholesaler who again would supply smaller orders to retail outlets.
- Retail outlets - you could market directly to the retailers.
- End users - these products can easily be supplied direct to the end user through mail order.

In addition to the normal considerations that we have discussed the following additional areas need to be understood.

- Quality can vary greatly so make sure that the quality matches the market you are trying to enter.
- The product must be adequately protected during transit.
- Import licenses may be required in the country of destination.
- These products can be produced very cheaply in the Far East owing to the low labor costs there - make sure your product can actually compete on price in the selected market.
- Certain specialized clothing products, for instance wool and linens will often be more successful than mass-produced items.

Generally speaking this is a good area for the new export agent as there is no great need of technical knowledge and there are fewer pitfalls than with engineering products.

12.7 Clothing - Import

There are some excellent sources of clothing products, for example India, Pakistan, Korea,

Thailand, Singapore etc. This is mainly due to the plentiful supplies of raw material and the very low labor costs in those countries. However, if you want to enter the exclusive and fashion markets you will need to look for suppliers in those countries that have specialized in these fields, for example France and Italy.

You have a number of choices with distribution channel - wholesaler, retailer, mail-order and even market traders.

The differences where the import of clothing products is concerned are as follows

- Is an import license required?
- What is the best method of transport?
- Do the products comply with any fire safety standards?
- What import duty rates will apply to these products?
- Is their quality equal to the market requirement?
- Do they need re-packing for presentation to the customers?

Again, this is a good product for the new agent to tackle as it is a fairly straightforward market

As we come to the end of this manual, I would like to thank you for following through. Good luck in creating a better place for you, yours and others.

Printed in Great Britain
by Amazon.co.uk, Ltd.,
Marston Gate.